Contents

How to use this book

Start by writing your name on the front cover – this workbook has been designed for you!

You can use it as you progress through your GCSE Religious Studies course, or as part of your revision for the final exam. It's full of different activities to help you learn by doing, not just reading.

This workbook covers Paper 1, which is Component 1: Catholic Christianity.

This refers to pages in this student book. You can go back to your student book to read about the topic in more depth.

Activity 1.1: The Trinity
SB pages 2–3

Working your way through these activities will help strengthen your understanding of some of the key topics in your GCSE course.

Follow the instructions and write your answers in the space provided.

_____

_____

_____

_____

_____

AQA Religious Studies B Catholic Christianity with Islam and Judaism

GCSE

Peter Wallace
Marianne Fleming
Peter Smith
David Worden
Series editor:
Cynthia Bartlett

OXFORD

There are lots of blank lines for you to write in your answers.

Key terms
SB pages 2–3

It's important to get to grips with some of the specialist language that we use when talking about religion. You will need to recognise these 'key terms' because they may turn up in an exam question. And you will also need to know how to use them in your answers. These activities will help you to feel confident using religious language. Test yourself regularly on these terms.

Key Terms Glossaries appear at the end of chapters 1 to 6.

Key Terms Glossary
You can collect the meanings of key terms here so you can refer to them at any time. You will also be creating a useful revision tool.

Sources of religious belief and teaching

 pages 2–3

The 5-mark question in the exam asks you to 'refer to scripture or another source of Christian belief and teaching.' These activities will help you to memorise short quotations from religious sources, such as the Bible, and also explain what these quotations mean.

This will also be helpful for the 4-mark and 12-mark questions because you can refer to religious teachings to add detail to the points you make, and to back up your arguments.

Exam practice

If you see an arrow running down the side of a box, that means the activity or activities you are doing will end with an exam practice question. These are like the questions that you will encounter in your exams. Use the information and guidance from the activities to practise the 1, 2, 4, 5 and 12-mark questions.

TIP

Keep an eye out for these TIPS. They contain useful advice, especially to help with your exam.

Finally, there is a whole chapter dedicated to

Exam practice

There are five different types of question in the AQA exam paper – the **1**, **2**, **4**, **5** and **12-mark** questions.

Work your way through this chapter to find out what each question will look like and how it is marked.

There are some activities that will help you to understand what the examiner is looking for in an answer, and activities that practise the skills you should be demonstrating. You should then be ready to have a go at a few questions yourself.

WHAT WILL THE QUESTION LOOK LIKE?

This explains the command words that the question will use.

HOW IS IT MARKED?

This explains what the examiner will be looking for in your answer.

 REMEMBER...

This provides useful tips to help raise your marks

All answers can be found online at **www.oxfordsecondary.co.uk/aqa-rs-answers**, so you can mark what you've done.

Once you have filled out this workbook, you will have made your own book to revise from. That's why your name is on the cover.

Chapter 1: **Creation**

Mark the following statements about Michelangelo's *Creation of Adam* as true or false.

	True	False
The *Creation of Adam* is a painting on the ceiling of the Sistine Chapel in Rome.	✓	
God is shown as a child in the painting.		✓
The painting represents the birth of Jesus.		✓
The painting represents the moment when God makes Adam come to life.	✓	
The painting reminds people that humanity is made in the image of God.	✓	
The painting represents God as the creator of life.	✓	
The painting shows that God and humans want a close relationship.	✓	
The painting shows Adam as an elderly man.		✓

Exam practice

Use your answers to Activity 1.1 above to help you answer the following question.

Give **two** ideas about God expressed in Michelangelo's *Creation of Adam*.   **[2 marks]**

1 _____

_____

2 _____

_____

TIP
You only need to give two simple points.

Activity 1.2: Other Christian art that depicts creation

 pages 12–13

This mosaic by Hildreth Meière can be found in St Bartholomew's church in New York. Fill in the sentences below about this mosaic using some of the words provided. (There are more words than gaps – you will have to decide which ones to leave out.)

large   lines   small   creator   abstract

hand   everything   all-knowing   wings

The American artist Meière created a mosaic showing the _____hand_____ of God in creation. It shows God's

hand as very _____large_____ compared to the size of the cloud above it. This suggests that God is powerful

and great. There are _____ extending to the edge of the circle. This shows that God created

_____ and his power and influence touch all things.

Meière's mosaic focuses on God as _____, not on God's relationship with humanity. It seems to

show that God continues to support and uphold the universe. Meière's mosaic is more _____ than

Michelangelo's *Creation of Adam*.

Key terms

pages 14–17

A These terms and their meanings are muddled up. Write out the meanings in the correct order in the second table.

Genesis 1	One who makes things
Genesis 2	God is outside and beyond life on earth and the universe
Omnipotent	Second chapter of Genesis, which describes how God created Adam and Eve
Creator	Almighty, having unlimited power
Transcendent	First chapter of Genesis, which describes how God created the universe in six days

Genesis 1	
Genesis 2	
Omnipotent	
Creator	
Transcendent	

B Now write the correct term beside each meaning. For an extra challenge, cover up the rest of this activity and try to see if you can recall the words from memory.

One who makes things	
First chapter of Genesis, which describes how God created the universe in six days	
God is outside and beyond life on earth and the universe	
Almighty, having unlimited power	
Second chapter of Genesis, which describes how God created Adam and Eve	

Activity 1.3: Creation and the nature of God in Genesis 1

 pages 14–15

The following statements are about God's nature in Genesis 1.
Copy each statement out into the correct box below. You will need to decide whether each statement shows that God is creator, God is transcendent, or God is omnipotent.

- God has the power to do whatever he wants.

- In Genesis 1, God creates everything in the universe, including humanity.

- God is outside and beyond creation, and only needs his own words to create.

- One quotation that supports this view is 'Then God said, "Let there be light"; and there was light' (Genesis 1:3, NRSV).

- All creation has been made by God.

- One quotation that supports this view is 'God saw everything he had made, and indeed it was very good' (Genesis 1:31, NRSV).

- Genesis 1 shows that God has the power to create things from nothing, exactly the way he wants them to be.

- God is beyond human understanding and cannot be fully described in human words.

- One quotation that supports this view is 'So God created humankind in his image' (Genesis 1:27, NRSV).

TIP

The words 'creator', 'transcendent' and 'omnipotent' may be used in exam questions, so try to remember what they mean. It will be helpful if you can use them correctly in your answers too.

God is creator

_____

_____

_____

_____

_____

_____

_____

_____

_____

God is transcendent

_____

_____

_____

_____

_____

_____

_____

_____

_____

God is omnipotent

_____

_____

_____

_____

_____

_____

_____

_____

_____

Exam practice

Now answer this exam question.

Explain **two** beliefs about the nature of God that are expressed in the creation story in Genesis 1.

Refer to scripture or another source of Christian belief and teaching in your answer. **[5 marks]**

_____

_____

_____

_____

_____

_____

_____

_____

_____

_____

_____

TIP

One of the five marks will be given for including a quotation from a source of Christian teaching (such as the Bible). Make sure the source you use is relevant to the point you are making.

Activity 1.4: The Genesis creation stories

 pages 14–17

There are two accounts of creation in Genesis, one in chapter 1 and the other in chapter 2.

Copy each statement into the correct column opposite, depending on whether you think they describe events in Genesis 1 or Genesis 2.

- God formed man out of the dust and breathed life into him.

- God made the first man, Adam.

- God created the world in six days.

- Adam named the animals that had been created by God.

- Eve was created to be a companion to Adam.

- The first thing that God created was light.

- The spirit of God hovered over the waters.

- This story shows that God created the world in an orderly way.

- God rested on the seventh day.

- God gave humans free will to choose whether to obey or disobey him.

Genesis 1	Genesis 2
• _____ _____	• _____ _____
• _____ _____	• _____ _____
• _____ _____	• _____ _____
• _____ _____	• _____ _____
• _____ _____	• _____ _____

Sources of religious belief and teaching

pages 14–17

Learn some quotations from Genesis 1 and 2.

A

" Then God said, 'Let there be light'; and there was light. "
Genesis 1:3, NRSV

This quotation shows that God created everything out of nothing, just by speaking his word (this is sometimes known as *ex nihilo*).

Fill in the gaps below. It will help you to learn the quotation if you say the whole thing out loud every time you write it.

" Then _____ said, 'Let there be _____'; and there was

_____. "

Now cover up the text above and have a go at writing out the whole quotation from memory.

" _____

_____ "

B

" So God created humankind in his image "
Genesis 1:27, NRSV

This quotation shows that humans share some qualities with God and that human life is sacred.

Fill in the gaps below to help you learn this second quotation.

" So _____ created _____ in his _____ "

Now cover up the text above and have a go at writing out the whole quotation from memory.

" _____ "

C

> " God saw everything that he had made, and indeed, it was very good. "
>
> *Genesis* 1:31, NRSV

This quotation shows that God is omnipotent (all-powerful) and benevolent (good). He can make creation perfect in every way.

Fill in the gaps below to help you learn this third quotation.

" _____ saw _____ that he had made, and indeed,

it was very _____ . "

Now cover up the text above and have a go at writing out the whole quotation from memory.

" _____

_____ "

D

> " the Lord God formed man from the dust "
>
> *Genesis* 2:7, NRSV

This quotation shows that God personally made the first man. It shows how precious humanity is.

Fill in the gaps below to help you learn this fourth quotation.

" the Lord _____ formed man from the _____ "

Now cover up the text above and have a go at writing out the whole quotation from memory.

" _____ "

E

> " Then the Lord God said, 'It is not good that the man should be alone' "
>
> *Genesis* 2:18, NRSV

This quotation shows that men and women need each other and are created to work together.

Fill in the gaps below to help you learn this fifth quotation.

" Then the Lord _____ said, 'It is not _____ that the man

should be _____ ' "

Now cover up the text above and have a go at writing out the whole quotation from memory.

" _____

_____ "

Activity 1.5: The significance of the creation stories for Catholics  pages 18–19

Tick the correct answer for each of the questions below.

1. What does Genesis teach about stewardship?

☐ People can treat creation in any way they want because God put them in charge of it.

☐ People have a duty to care for all of creation on behalf of God.

☐ People do not have to respect other species.

☐ Humans are the only species that should be respected.

2. What does Genesis teach about the dignity of human beings?

☐ Only believers should be treated with dignity.

☐ God does not care about human beings.

☐ Some people are created in God's image.

☐ Humans are made in the image of God and should be treated with dignity.

3. What does Genesis teach about free will?

☐ God gave humans free will so they can make decisions for themselves.

☐ Free will means believers have no choice about how they behave.

☐ God does not care how humans choose to act.

☐ Free will means God created the universe.

4. What does Genesis teach about the sanctity of life?

☐ How people treat others is not important.

☐ Catholics should respect life at every stage as it is a gift from God.

☐ God did not create humankind.

☐ Humans are in charge of creation.

Activity 1.6: The structure of the Bible

 pages 20–21

There are different types of writing in the Bible. The descriptions of these writings below are muddled up. Copy them into the correct box below to show whether they come from the Old Testament or the New Testament.

- The Gospels, which record the actions and teachings of Jesus.

- The Law, which show how the Jews became the people of God.

- The history books, which show how God guided his people.

- The Acts of the Apostles, which tell of some of the events of the early Church.

- The Epistles or letters, written to early Christians about how to follow Jesus' teachings.

- The wisdom books, which include poems, prayers and books of advice.

- The Book of Revelation, which some Christians believe describes the end of the world.

- The Prophets, containing the words of inspired people sent by God to teach his people about the faith.

Old Testament	New Testament
•	•
•	•
•	•
•	•

Exam practice

Now answer the exam question below.

Which **one** of the following can be found in the Old Testament of the Bible?　　　　**[1 mark]**

Put a tick (✔) in the box next to the correct answer.

A The Law.　　　□

B The Gospels.　　　□

C The Epistles.　　　□

D The Book of Revelation.　　　□

Activity 1.7: Inspiration and the Bible as the word of God　　　S B　pages 22–23

Fill in the gaps in these sentences about how the Bible was inspired by God, and how its interpretation is guided by God.

God i_____ the writers of the B_____ through the

H_____ S_____ .

Christians call the Bible the w_____ of God because they believe the Bible .

contains guidance and messages from G_____ .

God g_____ the Church as they decided which books should be accepted

into the B_____ .

The H_____ S_____ works through the bishops

who came after the apostles. The P_____ and bishops guide Catholics in

their interpretation of the Bible. This authority is known as the M_____ .

Key terms

pages 22–23

A These terms and their meanings are muddled up. Write out the meanings in the correct order in the second table below.

Term	Meaning
Apostles	The Third Person of the Trinity, who guides Christians today
Holy Spirit	Church leaders who are the successors to the apostles
Inspiration	Jesus' original followers sent out to teach the Christian message
Magisterium	Guidance that God gives to people
Bishops	The authority held by the Pope and bishops in the Catholic Church to help Christians understand the Bible

Term	Meaning
Apostles	
Holy Spirit	
Inspiration	
Magisterium	
Bishops	

B Now write the correct term beside each meaning. For an extra challenge, cover up the rest of this activity and try to see if you can recall the words from memory.

Meaning	Term
Church leaders who are the successors to the apostles	
The Third Person of the Trinity, who guides Christians today	
Jesus' original followers sent out to teach the Christian message	
The authority held by the Pope and bishops in the Catholic Church to help Christians understand the Bible	
Guidance that God gives to people	

Activity 1.8: Interpreting the Genesis creation stories

 pages 24–25

The following statements are muddled up. Copy them into the correct column of the table below depending on whether they are Catholic beliefs or fundamentalist beliefs.

- The creation stories can be accepted alongside scientific theories such as the theory of evolution.
- The creation stories are myths (stories that tell a deep truth or message but are not literally true).
- The Bible is accurate in every way.
- The creation stories should be interpreted literally.
- The world is only a few thousand years old.
- The main message of the creation stories is that God created everything.

TIP

Remember that 'interpretation' refers to how a text is read and understood.

Catholic interpretations of the Genesis creation stories	Fundamentalist interpretations of the Genesis creation stories
• _____	• _____
• _____	• _____
• _____	• _____

Activity 1.9: Natural law and Catholic attitudes towards science

pages 26–27

A Tick the correct answer for each of the questions below.

1. What is the basic natural law?

☐ Do good and avoid evil.   ☐ Do not steal.

☐ Do evil and avoid good.   ☐ Follow God.

2. Why does the Catholic Church believe that humans have an instinctive or natural knowledge of what it is to be good?

☐ They are intelligent.

☐ They can find guidance from the Bible.

☐ They are created in the image and likeness of God.

☐ They can follow the example of famous people such as politicians.

> **B** Mark the following statements about the Catholic Church and science as true or false.

	True	False
Catholics are not allowed to be scientists.	☐	☐
Catholics believe that scientists should help people to understand God's creation.	☐	☐
Friar Gregor Mendel is an example of a Catholic scientist.	☐	☐
Science is forbidden in the Bible.	☐	☐
Science tries to find out how things work.	☐	☐
Catholic bishops teach that people should not ignore religious viewpoints.	☐	☐

Activity 1.10: Caring for the environment

pages 28–29

There are three main reasons why Catholics should care for the environment. These are given in the boxes below.

Why are these reasons important? For each one, add two pieces of supporting evidence or further explanation. For example, refer to a Church teaching or Bible quotation, or explain why the reason is important. A couple have already been filled in for you.

Reason 1: Creation is special because it was made by God

- *Genesis 1 tells how God created the earth.*
- _____

Reason 2: God made humans to be stewards of the earth

- _____
- _____

Reason 3: It is part of treating others in a loving way

- *Pollution and climate change will affect all human life, so trying to prevent these is a way of showing love to all people.*
- _____

Exam practice

Now answer this exam question.

Explain **two** Catholic teachings about caring for the environment.   **[4 marks]**

_____

_____

_____

_____

> **TIP**
>
> Each reason should be made more detailed with a reference to a religious teaching, an example or extra information.

_____

_____

_____

_____

_____

_____

Activity 1.11: The meaning of stewardship   [S B] pages 30–31

Fill the gaps in the sentences below about stewardship using some of the words provided. (There are more words than gaps – you will have to decide which ones to leave out.)

Catholics	damage	environment	Bible	national	protect
God	local	government	Church	recycle	

Stewardship means that believers have the responsibility to look after the _____ on behalf of

_____ .

The Catholic Church teaches that it is important for all _____ to take real action to help

_____ the environment. For example, at a _____ level, Catholics can use public

transport more and _____ things instead of throwing them away.

At a _____ level, Catholics can put pressure on the

_____ to pass laws that are environmentally friendly.

Sources of religious belief and teaching

 page 31

Learn the following quotation from Pope Francis.

❝Everyone's talents and involvement are needed to redress the damage caused by human abuse of God's creation.❞

Pope Francis, Laudato Si 14

This quotation shows that the leader of the Catholic Church thinks it is important for everyone to help protect the environment.

TIP

You could explain this teaching in your own words in the exam.

Fill in the gaps below. It will help you to learn the quotation if you say the whole thing out loud every time you write it.

❝Everyone's _____ and _____ are needed to redress the

_____ caused by human _____ of God's creation.❞

❝Everyone's _____ and _____ are needed to

_____ the _____ caused by _____

abuse of _____ creation.❞

Now cover up the text above and have a go at writing out the whole quotation from memory.

❝_____

_____

_____❞

Key terms

 pages 30–33

A These terms and their meanings have been muddled up. Write out the meanings in the correct order in the second table below.

Stewardship	Able to provide everything that is needed without help from anyone else
Interdependence	The natural world, the surroundings in which we live
Self-sufficient	A relationship where both sides rely or depend on each other
Environment	A duty to look after the environment on behalf of God

Stewardship	
Interdependence	

Self-sufficient	
Environment	

B Now write the correct term beside each meaning. For an extra challenge, cover up the rest of this activity and try to see if you can recall the words from memory.

The natural world, the surroundings in which we live	
A relationship where both sides rely or depend on each other	
A duty to look after the environment on behalf of God	
Able to provide everything that is needed without help from anyone else	

Exam practice

Now answer the exam question below.

'For an individual Catholic, there is no point trying to save the environment.'

Evaluate this statement. In your answer you should:

- give reasoned arguments to support this statement
- give reasoned arguments to support a different point of view
- refer to Christian teaching
- reach a justified conclusion.

TIP

The answers you have written to Activity 1.10 as well as Activity 1.11 will help you write your answer here.

[12 marks]
[+3 SPaG marks]

 REMEMBER...

Focus your answer on the statement you are asked to evaluate.

- Try to write at least three paragraphs – one with arguments to support the statement, one with arguments to support a different point of view, and a final paragraph with a justified conclusion stating which side you think is more convincing, and why.
- Look at the bullet points in the question, and make sure you include everything that they ask for.
- The key skill that you need to demonstrate is evaluation. This means expressing judgements on the arguments that support or oppose the statement, based on evidence. You might decide an argument is strong because it is based on a source of religious belief and teaching, such as a teaching from the Bible, or because it is based on scientific evidence. You might decide an argument is weak because it is based on a personal opinion, or a popular idea with no scientific basis. You can use phrases in your chains of reasoning such as 'I think this a convincing argument because…' or 'In my opinion, this is a weak argument because…'.

_____
_____
_____
_____
_____
_____
_____
_____
_____
_____

Activity 1.12: CAFOD and sustainability

pages 32–33

Answer these questions in sentences.

1. What does 'sustainability' mean?

_____
_____

2. One example of sustainability is a company planting new trees to replace the ones that have been cut down to make their products. Give another example of sustainability.

_____
_____

3. What is CAFOD?

_____
_____

4. Give two examples of how CAFOD helps to support sustainability.

1 _____
_____
_____

2 _____
_____
_____

Key Terms Glossary

As you progress through the course, you can collect the meanings of key terms in the glossary below. You can then use the completed glossaries to revise from.

To do well in the exam you will need to understand these terms and include them in your answers. Tick the shaded circles to record how confident you feel. Use the extra boxes at the end to record any other terms that you have found difficult, along with their definitions.

○ **I recognise this term**

◐ **I understand what this term means**

● **I can use this term in a sentence**

Bible

CAFOD

Creation

Creation of Adam

Creator

Dignity

Environment

Free will

Gaudium et Spes

Genesis

Law

Magisterium _____

_____

_____

_____

_____

Stewardship _____

_____

_____

_____

_____

Natural law _____

_____

_____

_____

_____

Sustainability _____

_____

_____

_____

_____

Omnipotent _____

_____

_____

_____

_____

Transcendent _____

_____

_____

_____

_____

Prophecy _____

_____

_____

_____

_____

Word of God _____

_____

_____

_____

_____

Sanctity of life _____

_____

_____

_____

_____

_____

_____

_____

_____

Second Vatican Council _____

_____

_____

_____

_____

_____

_____

_____

_____

Chapter 2: **Incarnation**

Activity 2.1: Jesus as God incarnate

Tick the correct answer for each of the questions below.

1. Who visited Mary to announce that she would be the mother of Jesus?

☐ Angel Michael.

☐ Angel Gabriel.

☐ St Paul.

☐ St John.

2. What does the name 'Jesus' mean?

☐ Life force.

☐ Saviour.

☐ Bringer of good fortune.

☐ God with us.

3. What does 'Son of the Most High' refer to?

☐ A way of referring to the Holy Spirit.

☐ A way of referring to a political leader.

☐ A way of referring to God.

☐ A way of referring to children of political leaders.

4. What does 'incarnate' mean?

☐ A ghost.

☐ Being less than human.

☐ Someone who was an animal in their last life.

☐ God living as a human being.

Activity 2.2: God's message to Joseph
SB pages 38–39

Fill the gaps in the sentences below about God's message to Joseph using some of the words provided. (There are more words than gaps – you will have to decide which ones to leave out.)

God's		Jesus		shepherd		Matthew's
gold	angel	Holy	Joseph	Mary		

Luke's Gospel focuses more on _____. _____ Gospel focuses on Joseph who

is described as Mary's husband. Joseph is shown as being willing to obey _____ plan, however difficult

it might be. When _____ first heard about Mary's pregnancy, his plan was to break off the betrothal

(engagement) privately. Then an _____ appeared to him saying that the child had been conceived of

the _____ Spirit and his name was to be Jesus.

24

Activity 2.3: Jesus, the Word of God

 pages 40–41

A Read the opening section of John's Gospel below.

> **"** In the beginning was the Word, and the Word was with God and the Word was God. He was in the beginning with God. All things came into being through him and without him not one thing came into being. What has come into being with him was light, and the life was the light of all people. [...]
>
> And the Word became flesh and lived among us, and we have seen his glory, the glory as of a father's only son, full of grace and truth. **"**
>
> *John* 1:1–4; 14, NRSV

B Now answer the following questions in sentences.

1. How does the opening of John's Gospel remind readers of the beginning of the six-day creation story in Genesis 1?

   _____

   _____

   _____

   _____

2. Which words or phrases show the reader that Jesus is eternal?

   _____

   _____

   _____

3. Which words or phrases show the reader that Jesus was human?

   _____

   _____

   _____

4. 'The Word' refers to Jesus. Which words or phrases in this passage show Jesus is part of the Trinity?

   _____

   _____

   _____

   _____

Sources of religious belief and teaching

 pages 40–41

Learn some key quotations from John 1:1–14.

A

❝In the beginning was the Word, and the Word was with God, and the Word was God.❞

John 1:1, NRSV

This quotation shows that the Word (Jesus) is eternal and part of the Trinity.

Fill in the gaps below. It will help you to learn the quotation if you say the whole thing out loud every time you write it.

❝In the _____ was the Word, and the Word was with _____,

and the _____ was God.❞

❝In the beginning was the _____, and the _____ was with

God, and the Word was _____.❞

Now cover up the text above and have a go at writing out the whole quotation from memory.

❝_____

_____

_____❞

B

❝And the Word became flesh and lived among us❞

John 1:14, NRSV

The quotation shows that the Word (Jesus) became a human.

TIP

Whenever you write about the Word, if you follow it by 'Jesus' in brackets, you are showing you understand that John refers to Jesus as the Word.

Fill in the gaps below. It will help you to learn the quotation if you say the whole thing out loud every time you write it.

❝And the _____ became _____ and

_____ among us❞

❝_____ the Word _____ flesh and lived

_____ us❞

Now cover up the text above and have a go at writing out the whole quotation from memory.

❝_____

_____❞

Activity 2.4: Jesus as both fully human and fully God

pages 42–43

A Look at the diagram below. It shows Jesus was fully man and fully God.

Wept at the death of a friend

Ate and drank with all sorts of people

Suffered and died on the cross

Human

Jesus 'Son of Man'

Divine (fully God)

Asked at trial 'Are you the Messiah, the Son of the Blessed One?' He replied 'I am'.

(*Mark* 14:61–62, NRSV)

Resurrection proves that Jesus was always God – but during his time on Earth he lived as a human.

He was 'Son of Man' – someone who was completely human – in his relationships with his family and friends, in his physical needs such as food and water and because he suffered terrible pain as he died.

He was also 'Son of Man' – someone who has special authority from God – as shown when asked at his trial whether he was the Messiah, the Son of the Blessed One, he replied, 'I am'. This is the phrase God used to reveal himself to Moses.

B Mark the following statements about Jesus as true or false.

	True	False
Jesus was someone who never showed his emotions.	☐	☐
When Jesus was asked at his trial whether he was the Messiah, the Son of God, he replied, 'I am'.	☐	☐
Jesus uses the words 'I am' to show that he thinks he is important.	☐	☐
The resurrection shows Jesus was fully God.	☐	☐
Catholics believe that Jesus did not really die on the cross.	☐	☐
Jesus was a type of superhero who did not need to eat or drink.	☐	☐
'Son of Man' is used to show Jesus felt human emotions and suffered as a human being.	☐	☐
'Son of Man' is used to explain the special authority given to Jesus by God.	☐	☐

Key terms

pages 36–43

A These terms and their meanings are muddled up. Write out the meanings in the correct order in the second table below.

Incarnation	Official Church teaching
Grace	God becoming a human in Jesus
Eternal	God's free gift of unconditional love to believers
Doctrine	A Jewish name meaning 'God with us'
Word of God	When Angel Gabriel asked Mary to accept being the mother of Jesus
Emmanuel	A title referring to either just a human being or to a human given power by God
Annunciation	Second person of the Trinity – Jesus
Son of Man	Without beginning or end

Incarnation	
Grace	
Eternal	
Doctrine	
Word of God	
Emmanuel	
Annunciation	
Son of Man	

B Now write the correct term beside each meaning. For an extra challenge, cover up the rest of this activity and try to see if you can recall the words from memory.

Official Church teaching	
God becoming a human in Jesus	
God's free gift of unconditional love to believers	
A Jewish name meaning 'God with us'	
When Angel Gabriel asked Mary to accept being the mother of Jesus	
A title referring to either just a human being or to a human given power by God	
Second person of the Trinity – Jesus	
Without beginning or end	

Sources of religious belief and teaching
SB page 43

Learn this key quotation from Mark.

A

"'Are you the Messiah, the Son of the Blessed One?' Jesus said, 'I am'."

Mark 14:61–62, NRSV

This quotation from Mark 14 shows that Jesus was asked whether he was the Son of God (the Blessed One) and he answered by saying 'I am', the words that God used himself to Moses.

Fill in the gaps below. It will help you to learn the quotation if you say the whole thing out loud every time you write it.

"'Are you the _____, the Son of the _____ One?'

Jesus said, '_____'."

"'_____ you the Messiah, the _____ of the Blessed

_____?' _____ said 'I am'."

Now cover up the text above and have a go at writing out the whole quotation from memory.

"_____

_____"

Activity 2.5: Christian symbols

 pages 44–45

The following statements are muddled up. Copy them into the correct part of the table below. Two have been added for you.

- Sometimes worn as an alternative to a cross or crucifix to express faith.

- A secret symbol used by early Christians, meaning 'Jesus Christ, Son of God, Saviour'.

- The first and last letters of the Greek alphabet.

- A symbol made from the first two letters of the Greek word for Christ and a reminder of Jesus' death.

Symbol	Meaning	How the symbol is used by Catholics today
Ichthus (Fish)		*Often used in modern life to give a clear indication of Christian belief, for example as a bumper sticker or part of a business logo.*
Chi Rho		
Alpha and Omega		*Used on the Paschal candle and other church decorations to show God and Jesus are involved in everything, beginning to end.*

Exam practice

Now answer this exam question.

What **one** of the following does the Alpha and Omega symbolise? **[1 mark]**

Put a tick (✓) in the box next to the correct answer.

A A secret symbol meaning Jesus Christ, Son of God, Saviour. ☐

B An alternative to a cross. ☐

C A reminder of how Jesus died. ☐

D The first and last letters of the Greek alphabet showing God is involved in everything. ☐

Activity 2.6: How the incarnation affects Catholic attitudes towards religious art pages 46–47

A Copy the reasons for and against religious art into the correct column of the table below.

- God took on the human condition in Jesus, so we can reflect God in this form.
- The second commandment forbids making statues or artistic representations of God.
- Jesus can be shown as any ethnicity, helping understanding that Jesus offers salvation to all.
- Artistic representations of God can help people pray.
- When people pray in front of a statue, it may give the impression the statue is being worshipped.
- Some statues and pictures give a wrong impression, e.g. God is an old man with a beard.

For religious art	Against religious art
•	•
•	•
•	•

B Fill the gaps in the sentences below about religious art using some of the words provided. (There are more words than gaps – you will have to decide which ones to leave out.)

Jesus   mosaic   incarnation   statues   prayer   human

For many Catholics, the _____ gives a wonderful opportunity to portray God. As the incarnation shows

us God taking on the human condition in _____ , we can show him in a human form. Representations

of Jesus can show him as a man with all the qualities of a _____ . People can use these images and

statues as a focus for _____ .

Exam practice

Use your answers to Activity 2.6 to help you answer the following exam question.

Explain **two** ways the incarnation influences Catholic attitudes to religious art.　　　　**[4 marks]**

_____

_____

_____

_____

_____

_____

_____

_____

_____

_____

TIP

Don't just identify two different ways – give an extra detail or piece of information for each way to make sure you are explaining them to gain full marks.

Activity 2.7: Interpreting representations of Jesus

pages 48–49

A Fill in the labels on the picture of the Sacred Heart statue of Jesus below with these statements.

- One of Jesus' hands pointing to his heart, to draw attention to it.
- An expression of peace and love on Jesus' face.
- A crown of thorns.
- Flames coming from the heart representing Jesus' burning love.
- Holes in his hands from where Jesus was nailed to the cross.
- A hole or piercing through the heart representing where the soldiers pierced it with a sword.

B Mark the following statements about the crucifix as true or false.

	True	False
A crucifix is a representation of Jesus on the cross on which he died.	☐	☐
A crucifix is an empty cross.	☐	☐
The crucifix is a reminder of the love of God poured out in Jesus.	☐	☐
Jesus is dressed in kingly robes on some crucifixes.	☐	☐
A crucifix is a reminder of Jesus' resurrection.	☐	☐
Another word for a crucifix is an ichthus.	☐	☐

Exam practice

Now answer this exam question.

Give **two** Christian views about statues of Jesus. **[2 marks]**

1 _____

_____

2 _____

_____

Activity 2.8: The moral teachings of Jesus

pages 50–51

Jesus gave a talk called the Sermon on the Mount to his followers. The first part of it is a list of statements called the Beatitudes (*Matthew* 5:1–11, NRSV).

A Which of the statements below are from the Beatitudes? Tick the correct column for each one.

	✔	✗	?
Blessed are the meek, for they will inherit the earth.	☐	☐	☐
Blessed are the greedy, for they will inherit all wealth.	☐	☐	☐
Blessed are the lazy, for they will live a life of ease.	☐	☐	☐
Blessed are the pure in heart, for they will see God.	☐	☐	☐
Blessed are the aggressive ones, for they will be feared.	☐	☐	☐
Blessed are the merciful, for they will receive mercy.	☐	☐	☐

B Read the following text.

In the Parable of the Sheep and the Goats, Jesus tells his followers that it is important to care for people in need. Christians who help others will be rewarded with eternal life in heaven.

> **"** for I was hungry and you gave me food, I was thirsty and you gave me something to drink, I was a stranger and you welcomed me, I was naked and you gave me clothing, I was sick and you took care of me, I was in prison and you visited me. **"**
>
> *Matthew 25:35–36, NRSV*

TIP A phrase from the Parable of the Sheep and the Goats, e.g. 'I was hungry and you gave me food' will be a useful quotation in your exam to show an example of Jesus' teaching about how to treat others.

C Now answer the questions below in sentences.

1. Give three practical examples from the Parable of the Sheep and the Goats of ways that Christians can help others.

_____

_____

_____

2. What other ways can Christians help others today? Give two practical examples of your own.

_____

_____

_____

_____

Exam practice

Now answer this exam question. Use your answers to Activity 2.8 and the quotation you studied there to help you.

Explain **two** ways Christians should behave towards other people.

Refer to scripture or another source of Christian belief and teaching in your answer.

[5 marks]

TIP Make sure the scripture or teaching you refer to is clearly linked to the topic of the question. Using phrases like 'this is demonstrated in the quotation ...' can be helpful.

_____

_____

_____

_____

_____

_____

_____

_____

_____

_____

_____

_____

Activity 2.9: Tradition and St Irenaeus' writings about Jesus

pages 52–53

A Read the text below about tradition and St Irenaeus.

The teaching of the Catholic Church through the centuries is very important. There are some teachers who Catholics believe were inspired by the Holy Spirit. One such teacher was St Irenaeus.

St Irenaeus wrote Against Heresies (*Adversus Haereses*). A heresy is a belief that goes against the accepted teaching of the Church. Against Heresies explains that God is invisible and beyond human understanding. Jesus, who was with God from the beginning spoke as the Word through the prophets in Old Testament times.

Christians can get to know something of what God is like through Jesus. As Jesus is the Son of God, he displays God's character and qualities. Humans can understand God's nature better by looking at the life and actions of Jesus. Jesus, who is fully God and fully human is a meeting place between God and humanity.

Through the incarnation, God became part of humanity; God's glory became a human person in Jesus who lived a life totally open to the working of God in his life. Irenaeus used the phrase, 'the glory of God is a human being, fully alive' to explain this.

> **TIP**
> Look at Units 2.3 and 2.4 in the Student Book: they will help you understand St Irenaeus' teaching.

B Now answer the following questions in sentences.

1. Why do Catholics think tradition is very important?

_____

_____

_____

2. Name a book St Irenaeus wrote.

_____

3. How does Jesus show humans what God is like?

_____

_____

4. Explain Irenaeus' phrase, 'the glory of God is a human being, fully alive'.

_____

_____

_____

> **TIP**
> 'the glory of God is a human being, fully alive' is a quotation you could use in your exam.

Activity 2.10: Different understandings of the incarnation

 pages 54–55

A Read the text below.

The Magisterium explained how Jesus is fully man and fully God in *Verbum Dominum 12* and *Dei Verbum 4* (these are both documents issued by the Church). *Verbum Dominum* includes the quotation, 'The Son himself is the Word, the Logos: the eternal word became small – small enough to fit into a manger'. This shows it is a heresy (a teaching against the doctrine of the Church) to believe that Jesus was God and only pretended to be man. *Dei Verbum 4* explains that the Word was made flesh was sent 'as a man to men' and it is a heresy to teach that Jesus was just a very good man pretending to be God.

B Mark the following statements about the incarnation as true or false.

	True	False
It is a heresy to believe that Jesus was only a good man.	☐	☐
Catholic doctrine states that Jesus is both fully man and fully God.	☐	☐
Catholic doctrine states that Jesus was not really a proper human.	☐	☐
The Magisterium teaches that 'the eternal Word became small – small enough to fit into a manger'.	☐	☐
The Magisterium teaches that Jesus was the Word made flesh (human).	☐	☐
It is heresy to believe that Jesus was 'the Word sent as a man to men.'	☐	☐

Exam practice

Answer this exam question.

'A Catholic does not need to believe in the incarnation.'

Evaluate this statement. In your answer you should:

- give reasoned arguments to support this statement
- give reasoned arguments to support a different point of view
- refer to Christian teaching
- reach a justified conclusion.

TIP

Read through Units 2.3, 2.4 and 2.9 in the Student Book to help you think about two points of view and Catholic teaching.

[12 marks]
[+3 SPaG marks]

(!) REMEMBER...

Focus your answer on the statement you are asked to evaluate.

- Try to write at least three paragraphs – one with arguments to support the statement, one with arguments to support a different point of view, and a final paragraph with a justified conclusion stating which side you think is more convincing, and why.
- Look at the bullet points in the question, and make sure you include everything that they ask for.
- The key skill that you need to demonstrate is evaluation. This means expressing judgements on the arguments that support or oppose the statement, based on evidence. You might decide an argument is strong because it is based on a source of religious belief and teaching, such as a teaching from the Bible, or because it is based on scientific evidence. You might decide an argument is weak because it is based on a personal opinion, or a popular idea with no scientific basis. You can use phrases in your chains of reasoning such as 'I think this a convincing argument because…' or 'In my opinion, this is a weak argument because…'.

_____

_____

_____

_____

_____

_____

_____

_____

_____

_____

_____

_____

_____

_____

_____

_____

_____

Activity 2.11: Grace and the sacramental nature of reality

SB pages 56–57

A Look at this diagram showing different ways to explain the meaning of grace.

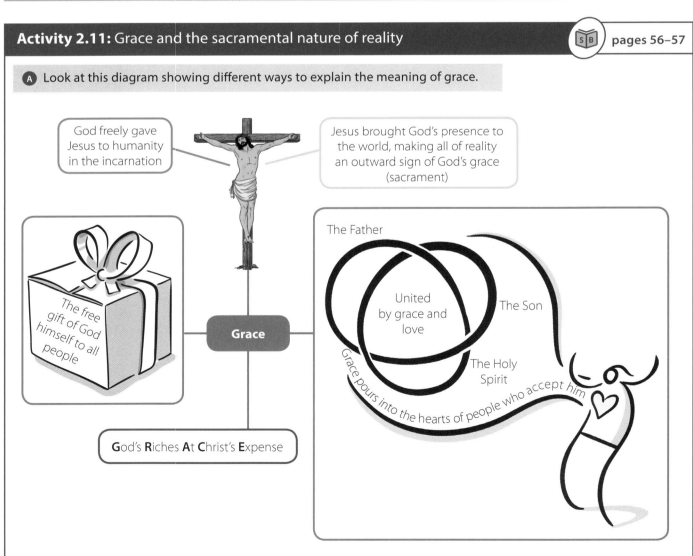

God freely gave Jesus to humanity in the incarnation

Jesus brought God's presence to the world, making all of reality an outward sign of God's grace (sacrament)

The free gift of God himself to all people

Grace

God's **R**iches **A**t **C**hrist's **E**xpense

The Father

United by grace and love

The Son

The Holy Spirit

Grace pours into the hearts of people who accept him

B Now fill the gaps in the sentences below about grace using some of the words and phrases provided. (There are more words than gaps – you will have to decide which ones to leave out.)

creation   sinful   sacraments   Son   sacrament
grace   divine   church   incarnation   love

Christians believe that grace comes from God, from the _____ between the three persons of

the Trinity, the Father, the _____ and the Holy Spirit – the _____ life. The

_____ (God taking on humanity in Jesus) shows God's _____ towards the

human race. Each person is sinful, yet through grace, God calls each person to a deeper relationship with him.

As Jesus came into the world, the whole of reality has become a _____ (an outward sign of God's grace

to humanity). Catholics have seven special rites and rituals which are called _____ because through

them, believers receive a special gift of grace.

C Look at the diagram below and then answer the questions in sentences.

Before the incarnation, God was seen as a distant (though caring) being.

Jesus was the ultimate gift from God to show his love for humanity.

Even though Jesus is no longer present on earth, the Holy Spirit is still active, sharing God's love with all people.

Since Jesus has lived on earth, people can see God as a living and active presence.

Jesus helped to bring God's love and presence into the world. This makes the world sacramental in nature.

1. How did the incarnation change how Christians see God?

_____

2. How do Christians believe God's spirit is working in the world today?

_____

3. How did Jesus make the world sacramental?

_____

Activity 2.12: The seven sacraments

 pages 58–59

The following statements about the seven sacraments are muddled up. Identify whether each of them is an action or an effect, then add it to the table in the correct place. Some have been done for you.

- When a person receives the consecrated Bread and Wine, the Body and Blood of Christ.

- Their forehead is anointed with holy oil.

- When a person who is very ill is anointed with holy oil.

- When a person becomes a member of the Church.

- Only happens once in a person's life.

- He is given certain powers such as being able to consecrate at Mass.

- Can happen regularly during Mass.

- When a person becomes a deacon, priest or bishop.

- The couple accept that, through their love for each other, the love of God is active in their lives.

- When a person confesses their sins to a priest and these are forgiven.

- When a man and a woman give their consent to be married.

- Water is poured on a person's head – symbolises washing away sin.

- The person becomes a child of God.

Sacrament	Action	Effect
Baptism	• • • Only happens once in a person's life.	•
Confirmation	• When a person chooses to confirm for themselves they are a member of the Church. • •	• The person's faith is strengthened and deepened. • The power of the Holy Spirit is renewed in their life.
Eucharist	• •	• This helps them keep growing in God's love.

Marriage	•	•
	• Usually only happens once in a person's life.	
Ordination	•	• The person commits himself to God and the Church.
	• Happens through the laying on of hands and the anointing of the hands with chrism (holy oil).	•
	• For each position can only happen once in a person's life.	
Reconciliation	•	• The person's relationship with God is restored.
	• Can happen regularly.	
Sacrament of the sick	•	• Gives strength to a person and also forgives their sins.

Activity 2.13: *Imago Dei* and abortion

S B pages 60–61

Answer the following questions in sentences.

1. What does *Imago Dei* mean?

_____

2. When do Catholics believe life begins?

_____

3. What did Elizabeth's unborn baby, John the Baptist, do when his mother met her cousin Mary who was pregnant with Jesus?

_____

_____

4. How might Catholics help protect unborn children?

_____

_____

Key Terms Glossary

As you progress through the course, you can collect the meanings of key terms in the glossary below. You can then use the completed glossaries to revise from.

To do well in the exam you will need to understand these terms and include them in your answers. Tick the shaded circles to record how confident you feel.

○ **I recognise this term**

◐ **I understand what this term means**

● **I can use this term in a sentence**

Alpha and Omega _____

Baptism _____

Beatitudes _____

Chi-Rho _____

Confirmation _____

Dei Verbum _____

Divine Word (Word of God) _____

Eucharist _____

Grace _____

Ichthus (fish) _____

Imago dei _____

Incarnate Son

Sacrament of the sick

Incarnation

Sanctification

Marriage

Son of Man

Ordination

Son of God

Reconciliation

Symbol

Sacrament

Verbum Domini

Chapter 3: **The Triune God**

Activity 3.1: The value of music in worship

pages 64–65

Fill the gaps in the sentences below about the value of music using some of the words provided.
(There are more words than gaps – you will have to decide which ones to leave out.)

involved	difficulty	beauty	the Bible
exclusive	joyful	unites	God

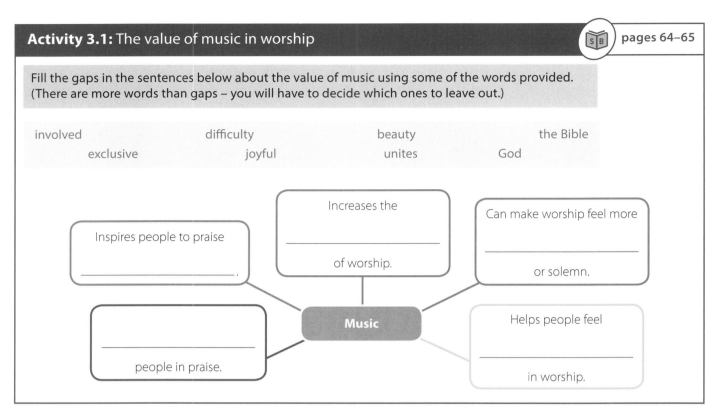

Inspires people to praise
_____ .

Increases the
_____
of worship.

Can make worship feel more
_____
or solemn.

Music

_____
people in praise.

Helps people feel
_____
in worship.

Activity 3.2: Music in the liturgy

pages 65–67

Answer the questions in the table below about the different types of music used in worship.
Some have already been filled in for you.

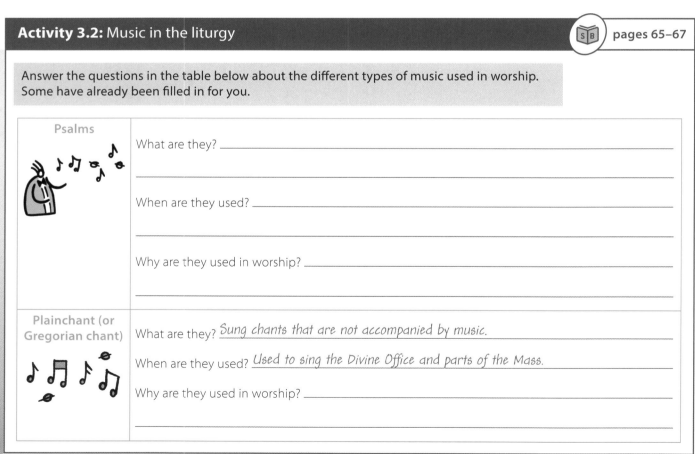

Psalms	What are they? _____
	When are they used? _____
	Why are they used in worship? _____
Plainchant (or Gregorian chant)	What are they? _Sung chants that are not accompanied by music._
	When are they used? _Used to sing the Divine Office and parts of the Mass._
	Why are they used in worship? _____

Traditional hymns	What are they? _____
	_____
	When are they used? _____
	_____
	Why are they used in worship? _They have stood the test of time, and help people to feel involved_
	in worship.
Contemporary worship songs	What are they? _____
	_____
	When are they used? _____
	_____
	Why are they used in worship? _____
	_____
Mass settings	What are they? _____
	_____
	When are they used? _____
	_____
	Why are they used in worship? _____
	_____

Exam practice

Now answer the following exam question.

Which **one** of the following correctly describes the psalms?   **[1 mark]**

Put a tick (✓) in the box next to the correct answer.

A Modern songs written to praise God.   ☐

B Poems included in the Bible.   ☐

C Music for the organ to be played at the end of services.   ☐

D Stories told by Jesus.   ☐

Activity 3.3: Acclamations used in the Mass

 pages 68–69

A Read the following text about the acclamations used in the Mass.

The acclamations are specific parts of the Mass that highlight the praise and celebration of God. They are often set to music.

- The **Gloria** is a great hymn of praise to God near the beginning of the Mass. It is not used in penitential seasons such as Advent and Lent.

- **Alleluia** is a Hebrew word which means 'praise God'. It is used to introduce the Gospel reading, to greet the presence of Christ. It is not used during Lent.

- **Sanctus** is a Latin word meaning 'holy'. This hymn is sung just before the Eucharistic prayer and it praises God's holiness.

- The **Mystery of Faith** is an acclamation directly after the consecration. In these words, everyone proclaims that they accept that the consecration has made present the whole saving event of Christ's life, death and resurrection.

TIP

The consecration is when the bread and wine are blessed and Catholics believe they become the actual Body and Blood of Christ. In this way Jesus is then present in the Mass. When Catholics declare the Mystery of Faith they are acknowledging to Jesus that they believe his life, death and resurrection have saved them and shown them God's love.

B Now answer the following questions in your own words.

1. What is the Gloria?

_____

_____

2. Why is the Gloria not sung during Lent?

_____

3. What does the word 'Alleluia' mean?

_____

4. Who is praised in the Sanctus?

_____

5. What is the Mystery of Faith?

_____

_____

6. Which acclamation is used to introduce the Gospel reading, except during Lent?

_____

_____

TIP

Listening to examples of each acclamation will help you remember which is which.

Exam practice

Now answer the following exam question.

Explain how **two** acclamations in the Mass highlight the praise and celebration of God.　　**[4 marks]**

_____

_____

_____

_____

_____

_____

_____

_____

_____

_____

TIP

Remember to give extra detail for each example to gain full marks.

Sources of religious belief and teaching

pages 70–71

A　Learn some quotations connected to the Triune God and the Trinity.

> **The Lord is our God, the Lord alone.**
> *Deuteronomy* 6:4, NRSV

This quotation shows that there is only one God. It is part of a Jewish prayer called the Shema.

Fill in the gaps below. It will help you to learn the quotation if you say the whole thing out loud every time you write it.

"The _____ is our _____, the Lord _____."

Now cover up the text above and have a go at writing out the whole quotation from memory.

"_____"

❝he saw the Spirit of God descending like a dove […] And a voice from heaven said, 'This is my Son'**❞**
Matthew 3:16–17, NRSV

This quotation is about the baptism of Jesus. It shows that God is three persons (Father, Son and Holy Spirit). It teaches Christians that the three persons are separate to each other, and can act independently of each other.

Fill in the gaps below to help you learn this second quotation.

❝he saw the _____ of God _____ like a _____ […]

And a _____ from _____ said, 'This is my _____'**❞**

Now cover up the text above and have a go at writing out the whole quotation from memory.

❝_____

_____

_____**❞**

B Now answer the following questions about the quotations you have just learned.

1. Christians believe that although God is three persons, there is still only one God. Write out a quotation from the Bible that supports this belief.

   _____

   _____

   _____

TIP If you use these quotations in your exam, mention that they come from the Bible, but don't worry about saying which specific book and chapter they come from. If you can't remember a quotation word-for-word, putting it in your own words (paraphrasing) can still be very useful.

2. How is the Holy Spirit described in the account of Jesus' baptism?

   _____

3. What does the account of Jesus' baptism teach Christians about the Trinity?

   _____

   _____

   _____

Activity 3.4: The Trinity in the Nicene Creed   📖 pages 72–73

Mark the following statements about the Nicene Creed as true or false.

	True	False
The Nicene Creed teaches that:		
There are two persons of the Trinity.	☐	☐
God the Father is the creator of all life.	☐	☐

	True	False
The Son of God, Jesus, was only a human – not God at all.	☐	☐
The Son of God, Jesus, is really God and has exactly the same nature as God.	☐	☐
The Holy Spirit is equal to the Father and the Son.	☐	☐
The Holy Spirit inspires people to let them know what God wants.	☐	☐
Only God the Father is eternal – the Son and Holy Spirit are not.	☐	☐

Activity 3.5: The Trinity in Genesis 1:1–3

SB page 73

A Read the following quotation.

> "In the beginning when God created the heavens and the earth, the earth was a formless void and darkness covered the face of the deep, while a wind swept over the face of the waters. Then God said, "Let there be light"; and there was light. "
> *Genesis* 1:1–3, NRSV

B Now answer the following questions.

1. When Christians read 'In the beginning when God created the heavens', which person of the Trinity do they think this refers to?

   _____

2. Genesis 1:1–3 describes a wind sweeping over the waters. Which person of the Trinity is this talking about?

   _____

3. God used the power of his Word to create the universe. Which person of the Trinity is this talking about?

   _____

4. What does Genesis 1:1–3 teach Christians? Tick the correct answer.

   God created the universe by using his hands. ☐

   All three persons of the Trinity were involved in the creation of the universe. ☐

   The Father is the only person of the Trinity who is eternal. ☐

   The Holy Spirit was not involved in creation. ☐

Activity 3.6: The influence of the Trinity on Christians today

pages 74–75

Fill the gaps in the sentences below about the Trinity using the words provided.
(There are more words than gaps – you will have to decide which ones to leave out.)

sanctity   grace   Trinity   evangelism   baptism
Council   mission   the Pope   Jesus   Gospel

The love between the _____ flows outward into the lives of believers as _____.

Christians are inspired to pass on this love to others.

One way they do this is by going out into the world to care for others. This is called _____.

Another way they show love is by preaching the _____ – telling other people the good news about

_____ and how he can save them. This is called _____.

Exam practice

Now answer the following exam question.

Explain **two** Christian beliefs about the Trinity.   **[2 marks]**

1 _____

_____

2 _____

_____

Activity 3.7: The Trinity in the Bible

pages 76–77

Tick the correct answer for each of the questions below.

1. Which passage in the Bible mentions all three persons of the Trinity?

☐ The account of Jesus' death.   ☐ The account of Jesus' baptism.

☐ The parable of the good Samaritan.   ☐ The parable of sheep and the goats.

2. In this passage, how is the Father described?

☐ As a bright light.   ☐ As a ghost.

☐ As a burning bush.   ☐ As a voice from heaven.

3. Why is this account important to Christians?

☐   It teaches that the Father is more important than the Son and the Holy Spirit.

☐   It shows that Jesus, the Son, is more important than the Father and the Spirit.

☐   It confirms that God is three persons, and the three persons are separate to each other.

☐   It shows God the Spirit descending as a sparrow.

4. Galatians 4:6–7, NRSV, says that Christians are able to call God 'Abba'. What does this mean?

☐   Christians are children of God, so they can call God 'Father'.

☐   'Abba' means king.

☐   'Abba' means officer in charge.

☐   Christians are like sheep and God is their shepherd.

5. What does Galatians 4:6–7 teach about the Holy Spirit?

☐   God does not send his Spirit to believers.

☐   Only some Christians receive the Spirit.

☐   God sends the Spirit into believers' hearts.

☐   The Spirit is not part of God.

Activity 3.8: The Trinity and God's love

pages 78–79

A   **Look at this table to remind yourself about St Augustine's and Catherine LaCugna's teachings on the Trinity.**

St Augustine's explanation of the Trinity	Catherine LaCugna's explanation of the Trinity
Differences	
St Augustine focuses on the relationship *within* the Trinity. He said it is essential to understand that the Trinity is three persons who are united in love. This love is then shared with all people through the Holy Spirit.	Catharine LaCugna focuses on the Trinity's *outward* effects: how the Trinity affects people's lives. For example, she writes about how the Son came to earth to save humanity, and how the Holy Spirit guides people towards the Father.
Similarities	
• Both say that love is a very important part of the Trinity. • Both say the eternal relationship between the Father, Son and Holy Spirit is very important.	

B Now answer the following questions in your own words.

1. How are St Augustine's and Catherine LaCugna's explanations of the Trinity similar?

_____

_____

_____

_____

2. How are St Augustine's and Catherine LaCugna's explanations of the Trinity different?

_____

_____

_____

_____

Exam practice

Now answer the following exam question.

Explain **two** ways that Catholics describe the Trinity.

Refer to scripture or another source of Christian belief and teaching in your answer. **[5 marks]**

_____

_____

_____

_____

_____

_____

_____

_____

_____

_____

_____

_____

Activity 3.9: The authority of the Magisterium page 80

A Fill in the gaps in the diagram below about how the authority of the Magisterium was established.

Jesus' closest followers were the twelve a_____.

↓

The apostles chose other people to help lead the Church. Through the l_____

on of hands, they passed on their own a_____ and the power of the

H_____ Spirit. These people became known as b_____.

↓

The leader of the apostles, P_____, died in Rome. The Bishops of Rome

(the P_____) continued to lead the Catholic Church.

↓

Today, the Pope and the b_____ form the M_____:

the teaching authority of the Catholic Church.

B Now answer the following questions in your own words.

1. How was the authority of the apostles passed on to the bishops?

_____

_____

_____

_____

2. How is the current Pope connected to Peter?

_____

_____

_____

_____

_____

Activity 3.10: The Councils of Nicea and Constantinople

page 81

Mark the following statements about the Councils of Nicea and Constantinople as true or false.

	True	False
The Council of Nicea happened in the 20th century.	☐	☐
The Council of Constantinople discussed the views of a priest called Arius.	☐	☐
The Council of Nicea was a meeting of the bishops.	☐	☐
The Council of Nicea confirmed that the Father and the Son are equal and of the same nature.	☐	☐
The Council of Constantinople confirmed that the Holy Spirit is the third person of the Trinity and fully God.	☐	☐
The Council of Constantinople confirmed that Jesus is fully God but not fully human.	☐	☐

Activity 3.11: Baptism

pages 82–83

A Fill the gaps in the sentences below about baptism using the words provided. (There are more words than gaps – you will have to decide which ones to leave out.)

resurrection   death   name   God   disciples   grace   trial   sin
immersion   water   Spirit   oil   Christ   Church   Trinity

The early Christians would have been baptised by total _____ (going under the water completely). This

symbolises joining in with Jesus' _____. The believer commits their life to _____

in the same way that Christ did when he went to his death. Rising up out of the water symbolises joining in with Jesus'

_____, to start a new life as a Christian. Today in the Catholic Church, _____

is anointed on the person's head. This shows that the person is being filled with the Holy _____.

Baptism is a sign of initiation into the _____. The believer is cleansed of all _____

and becomes a child of the Father. People are baptised in the _____ of the Father, the Son and the Holy

Spirit. Through their baptism, they share in the life of the _____.

B Match these sentence beginnings and endings on the Trinity and baptism. Write out the full sentences in the boxes on the next page.

When Christians are baptised they become a child of	Jesus
When Christians are baptised they join in the death and resurrection of	the Holy Spirit
When Christians are baptised they are filled with	the Father

Activity 3.12: Traditional and spontaneous prayer

S B pages 84–85

A The following statements are muddled up. Copy them out into the correct column of the table below.

- Prayers with no set format or words.

- Prayers that have been passed down over the generations.

- An example is the 'Our Father'.

- People who use these prayers believe the Holy Spirit guides them in what to say.

- Allows people to talk about their own concerns and worries with God.

- Means people do not have to come up with their own words.

TIP
The Lord's Prayer can be used as a source of Christian belief and teaching in an answer to an exam question about prayer.

Traditional prayers	Spontaneous prayers
• _____	• _____
• _____	• _____
• _____	• _____

B Now answer the following questions.

1. One advantage of traditional prayers is given in the list above. Give one more advantage here:

_____

_____

_____

_____

2. One advantage of spontaneous prayers is given in the list above. Give one more advantage here:

_____

_____

_____

_____

3. Describe a situation when a Catholic might prefer to use traditional prayer rather than spontaneous prayer.

_____

_____

4. Now describe a situation when a Catholic might prefer to use spontaneous prayer rather than traditional prayer.

_____

_____

5. Here are some reasons why Catholics might prefer to use traditional prayer. Underline which you think is the strongest reason. (There is no correct answer as such – but you will need to explain your choice.)

- Traditional prayers are useful when people are upset and cannot think clearly.

- Traditional prayers make it easier to be open to the presence of God rather than worrying about the words.

- Using a traditional prayer means that someone is joining in with other Christians using that prayer around the world.

Give a reason for your choice:

_____

_____

_____

_____

Exam practice

Use your answers from Activity 3.12 to help you answer the following exam question.

'Catholics should only use traditional prayer to communicate with God.'

Evaluate this statement. In your answer you should:

- give reasoned arguments to support this statement
- give reasoned arguments to support a different point of view
- refer to Christian teaching
- reach a justified conclusion.

[12 marks]
[+3 SPaG marks]

 REMEMBER...

Focus your answer on the statement you are asked to evaluate.

- Try to write at least three paragraphs – one with arguments to support the statement, one with arguments to support a different point of view, and a final paragraph with a justified conclusion stating which side you think is more convincing, and why.

- Look at the bullet points in the question, and make sure you include everything that they ask for.

- The key skill that you need to demonstrate is evaluation. This means expressing judgements on the arguments that support or oppose the statement, based on evidence. You might decide an argument is strong because it is based on a source of religious belief and teaching, such as a teaching from the Bible, or because it is based on scientific evidence. You might decide an argument is weak because it is based on a personal opinion, or a popular idea with no scientific basis. You can use phrases in your chains of reasoning such as 'I think this a convincing argument because…' or 'In my opinion, this is a weak argument because…'.

_____
_____
_____
_____
_____
_____
_____
_____
_____
_____
_____
_____
_____

Activity 3.13: Prayer and posture

S B pages 86–87

Which postures are being described in the table below? Write your answers in the second column. Use each of the following postures once.

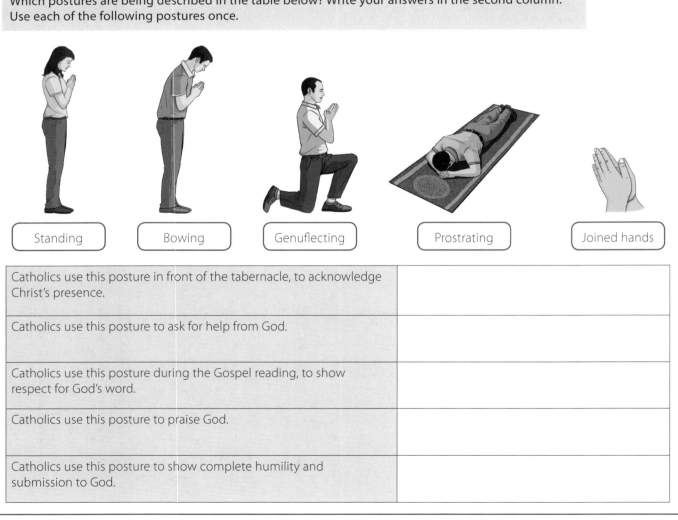

| Standing | Bowing | Genuflecting | Prostrating | Joined hands |

Catholics use this posture in front of the tabernacle, to acknowledge Christ's presence.	
Catholics use this posture to ask for help from God.	
Catholics use this posture during the Gospel reading, to show respect for God's word.	
Catholics use this posture to praise God.	
Catholics use this posture to show complete humility and submission to God.	

Key terms

S B pages 64–87

A Some of the key terms that you should know for this chapter are given below, but the terms and their meanings are muddled up. Write out the meanings in the correct order in the second table below.

Mass (Eucharist)	A part of the Mass that people join in with saying or singing together
Acclamation	Sending out Christians to help others
The Trinity	The belief that the Father, Son and Holy Spirit are 'of one being' (they are one God)
Consubstantial	A ceremony that celebrates the sacrifice, death and resurrection of Jesus using bread and wine
Evangelism	The belief that there are three persons in one God
Mission	Preaching the good news about Jesus to other people

Mass (Eucharist)	
Acclamation	
The Trinity	
Consubstantial	
Evangelism	
Mission	

B Now write the correct term beside each meaning. For an extra challenge, cover up the rest of this activity and try to see if you can recall the words from memory.

The belief that the Father, Son and Holy Spirit are 'of one being' (they are one God)	
Sending out Christians to help others	
The belief that there are three persons in one God	
A part of the Mass that people join in with saying or singing together	
Preaching the good news about Jesus to other people	
A ceremony that celebrates the sacrifice, death and resurrection of Jesus using bread and wine	

Key Terms Glossary

As you progress through the course, you can collect the meanings of key terms in the glossary below. You can then use the completed glossaries to revise from.

To do well in the exam you will need to understand these terms and include them in your answers. Tick the shaded circles to record how confident you feel. Use the extra boxes at the end to record any other terms that you have found difficult, along with their definitions.

○ **I recognise this term**

◐ **I understand what this term means**

● **I can use this term in a sentence**

Council of Nicea _____

Acclamation _____

Doctrine _____

Alleluia _____

Evangelism _____

Catherine LaCugna _____

Gloria _____

Contemporary worship _____

God the Father _____

Council of Constantinople _____

God the Son _____

Holy Spirit _____

_____

_____

_____

_____

Nicene Creed _____

_____

_____

_____

_____

Initiation _____

_____

_____

_____

_____

Plainchant _____

_____

_____

_____

_____

Liturgy _____

_____

_____

_____

_____

Posture _____

_____

_____

_____

_____

Mass settings _____

_____

_____

_____

_____

Prayer _____

_____

_____

_____

_____

Mission _____

_____

_____

_____

_____

Psalms _____

_____

_____

_____

_____

Mystery of Faith _____

_____

_____

_____

_____

Sanctus _____

_____

_____

_____

_____

Spontaneous prayer _____

_____

_____

_____

_____

Worship _____

_____

_____

_____

_____

St Augustine _____

_____

_____

_____

_____

_____

_____

_____

_____

_____

Traditional hymns _____

_____

_____

_____

_____

_____

_____

_____

_____

_____

Traditional prayer _____

_____

_____

_____

_____

_____

_____

_____

_____

_____

Trinity _____

_____

_____

_____

_____

_____

_____

_____

_____

_____

Triune God _____

_____

_____

_____

_____

_____

_____

_____

_____

_____

Chapter 4: **Redemption**

 page 90

Fill the gaps in the sentences below about church architecture using some of the words provided.
(There are more words than gaps – you will have to decide which ones to leave out.)

altar	God	atrium	cathedrals	prayer
chapels	Eucharist (Mass)	worship	Pope	Christmas

For Catholics, the Church is the people of _____. A church is a building where people meet to

_____ God. The most important service is the _____. This is offered on the

_____, so this is the focus of the church's design. However, Catholic church buildings are also used for

quiet, personal _____. There are often side _____ set aside for this.

pages 90–91

The design of Catholic churches changed after the Second Vatican Council (1962–1965).

The following statements are muddled up. Copy them into the correct columns below, depending on
whether they describe churches built before or after 1965.

- Focused on allowing as many people as possible to see and join in with the Mass.
- Built facing towards Jerusalem.
- The altar is against the east wall, so the priest has his back to people.
- Built around the altar.
- The altar is sometimes physically in the middle of the building.
- Usually built in a cross shape.

Catholic churches built before 1965	Catholic churches built after 1965
• _____ _____	• _____ _____
• _____ _____	• _____ _____
• _____ _____	• _____ _____

Activity 4.3: The main parts of a Catholic church

 pages 92–93

Fill in the gaps in the sentences below about the main parts of a Catholic church.

The lectern	The B_____ readings are given from here. There are at least two readings at every M_____. Christians believe that Christ is truly present when the G_____ is read.
The altar	At Mass, people offer God b_____ and w_____ on the altar. When it is blessed, this offering is joined to C_____'s offering of himself to the Father through his death on the cross. Every Mass is absorbed into the great P_____ sacrifice (the Last Supper, death and resurrection of Jesus).
The crucifix	This is a cross that bears the image of J_____. It is a reminder that Jesus suffered to save h_____. It helps believers to be grateful for all Jesus has done.
The tabernacle	This is where the consecrated B_____ is kept for later use. Catholics believe that the tabernacle houses the R_____ P_____ of Christ. Catholics genuflect in front of it. Many Catholics also like to pray quietly in front of it.

Exam practice

Now answer the exam question below.

Which **one** of the following best explains what the altar is in a Catholic church?   **[1 mark]**

Put a tick (✔) in the box next to the correct answer.

A A place where baptisms happen.   ☐

B A place where the consecrated Bread is kept for later use.   ☐

C A place where the bread and wine are offered to God in the Mass.   ☐

D A statue of Mary.   ☐

Activity 4.4: Contrasting features and artefacts used by Catholics

S B   pages 94–95

Tick the correct answer for each of the questions below.

1. What is an altar?

☐ A place of sacrifice and thanksgiving.   ☐ The entrance to a church.

☐ A picture of Jesus.   ☐ A place where the last rites happen.

2. Why do some churches prefer to use a wooden table rather than an altar?

☐ It reminds people of the Trinity.

☐ A wooden table is used for animal sacrifices.

☐ It reminds Christians they are re-enacting the meal of the Last Supper.

☐ It reminds Christians of the natural world.

3. Why do many Catholic churches use crucifixes?

☐ It is a reminder that God is omnipotent.

☐ It represents the importance of caring for the environment.

☐ It is a reminder of all that Jesus suffered for humanity.

☐ It reminds believers of Mary.

4. Why do some Christians prefer to use a cross rather than a crucifix?

☐ Using a cross helps believers to focus more on Jesus' suffering and death.

☐ It does not include a figure of Jesus, so there is no suggestion of worshipping an idol.

☐ The cross is a symbol of the ascension.

☐ Only priests are allowed to wear a crucifix.

5. Why do some Christians believe the best image to use is the Risen Christ?

☐ It shows Jesus being crucified.

☐ It is a reminder of Jesus being born.

☐ It represents going on pilgrimage to heaven.

☐ It emphasises the importance of Jesus' resurrection.

Activity 4.5: The relationship between free will and sin

ⓢⓑ page 96

- God did this because he wants people to choose to follow him.

- Jesus was sent to earth to help restore this relationship.

- Because humans have free will, they are able to sin.

- But God also gave humans free will.

- Because humans sin, this has broken the relationship between God and humanity.

- God made all creation perfect.

- A sin is any action or thought that reject's God's will.

TIP

Try to decide on the correct order before writing out all of the statements in the flowchart. You could use a pencil to number the statements to get them in the right order.

The statements below are muddled up. Add them in the correct order to the flowchart, to explain how the existence of free will and sin broke the relationship between God, humanity and the whole of creation.

1 ☐

2 ☐

4 ☐

3 ☐

5 ☐

6 ☐

7 ☐

Activity 4.6: The death, resurrection and ascension of Jesus

 pages 96–97

Fill in the gaps in the sentences below about Jesus' death, resurrection and ascension using some of the words provided. (There are more words than gaps – you will have to decide which ones to leave out.)

Father   creation   birth   resurrected   humanity   cosmic   sin
obedient   Jesus   crucified   ascended   grace   death

Christians believe that Jesus was totally _____ to God. He showed this both in

his life and _____. Jesus' crucifixion helped to restore the relationship between

God and _____.

Jesus was _____ three days after he died. This destroyed the power of

death and _____. They still exist but believers can now overcome them.

Jesus' resurrection also restored the harmony of _____.

Jesus _____ to heaven 40 days after the resurrection, and took his place by the

side of the _____.

Jesus' resurrection and ascension have helped restore the _____ order.

Sources of religious belief and teaching

 page 103

Learn the following quotation about the importance of the resurrection.

❝If Christ has not been raised, your faith is futile and you are still in your sins.❞

1 Corinthians 15:17, NRSV

This quotation shows the importance of Christ's resurrection. Without the resurrection, life after death would not be possible.

Fill in the gaps below. It will help you to learn the quotation if you say the whole thing out loud as you write it.

❝If _____ has not been _____ , your _____

is futile and you are _____ in your _____.❞

Now cover up the text above and have a go at writing out the whole quotation from memory.

❝_____

_____❞

Activity 4.7: The significance of Jesus' death, burial, resurrection and ascension (S B) pages 98–99

Mark the following statements about Jesus' death, burial, resurrection and ascension as true or false.

	True	False
Christians believe that Jesus' death redeemed humanity.	☐	☐
Jesus did not forgive those who helped to crucify him.	☐	☐
Christians believe that when Jesus died and was buried, he joined everyone who had died before him.	☐	☐
Christians believe that Jesus' resurrection means there is no hope for life after death.	☐	☐
Catholics believe that Jesus' resurrection actually happened.	☐	☐
Jesus and all his disciples ascended to heaven together.	☐	☐
Christians believe the Holy Spirit came to be with believers soon after the ascension.	☐	☐

Exam practice

Now answer the following exam question.

Explain **two** beliefs about the resurrection of Jesus.

Refer to scripture or another source of Christian belief and teaching in your answer. **[5 marks]**

_____

_____

_____

_____

_____

_____

_____

_____

_____

_____

_____

TIP

You can refer to the quotation you learned opposite for your source of Christian belief and teaching, as long as it is relevant to the point you are trying to make.

Activity 4.8: Salvation (past, present and future)

 pages 100–101

A Look at the table below.

Salvation in the past	Salvation in the present	Salvation in the future
Salvation came through the death and resurrection of Jesus. It is a gift of grace from God.	Salvation is an ongoing process. Believers need to allow themselves to be guided by the Holy Spirit, who helps them to resist the temptation to sin.	Salvation will be completed at the end of time, when God's Kingdom is fully established and the power of sin and death are completely destroyed.
How is this reflected in the liturgy?		
The offering made by Christ on the cross is re-enacted in the Mass.	When believers take the Body and Blood of Christ in the Mass, Christ enters their lives, giving them grace and the strength to resist sin.	The Mass is a chance to experience what the heavenly banquet will be like (this is the celebration that will happen when salvation is complete).

B Now answer the following questions in your own words.

1. How did Christ bring salvation in the past?

_____

_____

_____

TIP 'Grace' is basically another way of saying 'God's gift of love'. It refers to God's love, which is a free gift that God gives to all believers.

2. How is this reflected in the Mass?

_____

_____

3. How does the Holy Spirit help Christians to work towards salvation?

_____

_____

4. In the Mass, how are Christians given the strength to resist sin?

_____

_____

5. What will happen at the end of time?

_____

_____

6. How do Catholics look forward to this in the Mass?

_____

_____

Key terms

 pages 96–105

A These terms and their meanings are muddled up. Write out the meanings in the correct order in the second table below.

Atonement	A term referring to the Last Supper, suffering, death and resurrection of Jesus
Redemption	Restoring the relationship between God and people through the life, death and resurrection of Jesus
Salvation	Making up for the wrongs done by other people, to bring humanity back into a relationship with God
Paschal sacrifice	Being saved from sin; freedom from sin

Atonement	
Redemption	
Salvation	
Paschal sacrifice	

B Now write the correct term beside each meaning. For an extra challenge, cover up the rest of this activity and try to see if you can recall the words from memory.

A term referring to the Last Supper, suffering, death and resurrection of Jesus	
Restoring the relationship between God and people through the life, death and resurrection of Jesus	
Making up for the wrongs done by other people, to bring humanity back into a relationship with God	
Being saved from sin; freedom from sin	

Sources of religious belief and teaching

pages 102–103

A Learn some quotations about redemption.

"**My God, my God, why have you forsaken me?**"
Mark 15:34, NRSV

This is what Jesus cried out at his crucifixion, and shows that he was suffering. But even though he knew he would suffer, he still showed total obedience to God. He set an **example** for all people to follow.

Fill in the gaps below. It will help you to learn the quotation if you say the whole thing out loud every time you write it.

"My _____ , my God, _____ have you

_____ me?"

Now cover up the text above and have a go at writing out the whole quotation from memory.

"_____"

"**And the curtain of the temple was torn in two**"
Mark 15:38, NRSV

When Jesus died, the curtain that separated the holiest part of the temple in Jerusalem from where people stood was torn in two. This shows that Jesus' death broke down the barrier between God and humanity, **restoring** their relationship.

Fill in the gaps below to help you learn this second quotation.

"And the _____ of the _____ was torn

in _____"

Now cover up the text above and have a go at writing out the whole quotation from memory.

"_____"

"**Jesus said to her, 'Do not hold onto me, because I have not yet ascended to the Father'.**"
John 20:17, NRSV

This quotation comes from the resurrection story. Jesus has been raised back to life and is talking to Mary. Jesus is **victorious** over death and has made it possible for humanity to overcome death.

Fill in the gaps below to help you learn this third quotation.

"Jesus said to her, 'Do not _____ onto me, because I have not yet

_____ to the _____'."

Now cover up the text above and have a go at writing out the whole quotation from memory.

"_____

_____"

B Now answer the following questions about the quotations you have just learned.

1. When Jesus died, the Bible says that 'the curtain of the temple was torn in two'. What does this show about God's relationship with humanity? Explain your answer.

_____

_____

_____

2. At his crucifixion, how did Jesus set an example for all people to follow? In your answer, refer to a quotation from the Bible.

_____

_____

_____

3. Why do Christians call Jesus 'the victor'?

_____

_____

_____

Activity 4.9: St Irenaeus' thoughts on salvation

page 105

Fill the gaps in the sentences below about St Irenaeus' ideas using some of the words provided. (There are more words than gaps – you will have to decide which ones to leave out.)

Adam   death   forgave   metaphor   Joseph   sacraments
obeyed   life   relationship   restored   poem

St Irenaeus used a _____ of two trees to help understand salvation.

He said that _____ and Eve disobeyed God by eating from the tree of

knowledge of good and evil. This broke the _____ between God and

humanity, and brought _____ into the world.

Jesus _____ God by dying on the tree (on a wooden cross), and this

_____ God's relationship with humanity. The tree of the cross brought

_____ by offering the possibility of eternal life in heaven to all people.

Activity 4.10: St Anselm's thoughts on salvation

page 105

A **One** of the statements below is false. Underline the one you think isn't true.

- To explain salvation, St Anselm used the metaphor of freeing a slave by paying money.

- St Anselm said that humanity became slaves to sin after Jesus died on the cross.

- In St Anselm's metaphor, Jesus' obedience to God 'paid a ransom' for the sins of all humans.

- St Anselm said that Jesus' death means humans are no longer 'slaves' to sin.

B Correct the false statement by writing out a sentence with the correct information.

_____

_____

_____

Activity 4.11: Comparing St Irenaeus and St Anselm

page 105

Salvation is the idea of being freed from sin. Look back at Activity 4.8 to remind yourself about how people gain salvation, then answer the following questions.

1. Do you think that St Irenaeus' metaphor or St Anselm's metaphor is more helpful to Christians in understanding salvation?

_____

_____

2. Why do you think your choice is better than the other metaphor?

_____

_____

_____

_____

_____

_____

_____

TIP

Each metaphor focuses on different parts of salvation. St Irenaeus mentions Adam and Eve, and says that Jesus' death brought life. St Anselm says that Jesus' death paid for humanity's sins, so humans are now free from sin. Which of these do you think helps to explain salvation best? Whichever you choose, make sure you can give a reason for your answer.

Exam practice

Using your answers to Activities 4.9, 4.10 and 4.11 to help you, answer the exam question below.

'The metaphor of being freed from slavery is the best way for Christians to understand salvation.'

Evaluate this statement. In your answer you should:

- give reasoned arguments to support this statement
- give reasoned arguments to support a different point of view
- refer to Christian teaching
- reach a justified conclusion.

[12 marks]
[+3 SPaG marks]

 REMEMBER...

Focus your answer on the statement you are asked to evaluate.

- Try to write at least three paragraphs – one with arguments to support the statement, one with arguments to support a different point of view, and a final paragraph with a justified conclusion stating which side you think is more convincing, and why.
- Look at the bullet points in the question, and make sure you include everything that they ask for.
- The key skill that you need to demonstrate is evaluation. This means expressing judgements on the arguments that support or oppose the statement, based on evidence. You might decide an argument is strong because it is based on a source of religious belief and teaching, such as a teaching from the Bible, or because it is based on scientific evidence. You might decide an argument is weak because it is based on a personal opinion, or a popular idea with no scientific basis. You can use phrases in your chains of reasoning such as 'I think this a convincing argument because…' or 'In my opinion, this is a weak argument because…'.

Activity 4.12: The importance of conscience for Christians **pages 106–107**

A Read this text explaining what conscience means to Christians.

Conscience tells people what is right and wrong and should be guided by Church teaching.

One person's conscience can inspire others.

Natural law means that all people are born knowing what is right and wrong.

Science means 'knowledge', so conscience means 'with knowledge' of right and wrong.

Conscience is made up of natural instincts (the 'natural law'), but these instincts have to be shaped and developed.

Ignoring conscience leads to feeling guilty.

Educating conscience is important, so people should listen to others.

Natural law tells humans to 'love good and avoid evil' (*Gaudium et Spes* 16).

Conscience is the voice of God in a person's heart and soul.

Educating conscience is important, so people should listen to Church teachings.

B Now answer the following questions.

1. In one sentence, explain what Christians think their conscience is.

_____

_____

2. Give two ways that a Christian's conscience can be educated.

1 _____

_____

2 _____

_____

3. Does the Catholic Church teach that Catholics can follow their conscience even if this goes against Church teachings? Explain your answer.

_____

_____

_____

_____

_____

4. What is the natural law?

_____

_____

Exam practice

Now answer the following exam question.

Give **two** reasons why Catholics should follow their conscience. **[2 marks]**

1 _____

_____

2 _____

_____

Activity 4.13: Redemption and the Mass

SB pages 108–109

Answer the following questions about the Mass and what it means to Catholics.

1. Why is there always a section from the Gospels in the readings?

_____

_____

2. What do the people give as a sign of thanksgiving in the offertory?

_____

3. During the Eucharistic prayer, how is the bread and wine referred to?

_____

4. The Blood represents the new covenant. What does 'covenant' mean?

_____

_____

5. What freedom does the Mass celebrate?

_____

_____

6. What do believers receive through taking Communion?

_____

_____

_____

7. Which is the most important part of the Mass in your opinion? Give a reason to support your opinion.

_____

_____

_____

_____

Activity 4.14: Different Christian understandings of the Eucharist   **pages 110–111**

Complete the sentences below explaining the similarities and differences in Christian beliefs and practices related to the Eucharist.

Similarities between Catholic and Orthodox Christians

Both believe that C_____ is fully p_____ in the consecrated Bread and Wine.

Differences between Catholic and Orthodox Christians

The Orthodox Eucharist is called the L_____. There is more emphasis on

symbolism and r_____ than in the Catholic Mass.

In the Orthodox Eucharist, the c_____ takes place behind the i_____ .

Similarities between Catholic and Anglican (Church of England) Christians

Some Anglicans share the Catholic belief that the bread and wine become the B_____

and B_____ of Christ.

Differences between Catholic and Anglican (Church of England) Christians

Many Anglicans believe the Spirit of C_____ is received when Communion is given.

The b_____ and w_____ do not literally become the Body and Blood of Christ,

but Christ is spiritually present.

Differences between Catholic and Quaker and Salvation Army Christians

These groups do not celebrate the E_____ at all. Instead they believe Christ is present

through the S_____ , who inspires their prayers and actions, and that the whole of life is a

s_____ (an outward sign of an inward grace).

Differences between Catholic and nonconformist Christians (e.g. Baptists)

Many nonconformists believe the Eucharist is a memorial of Jesus' L_____ S_____

(so the Eucharist is held to remember it, not re-enact it).

Many believe that C_____ is present in the readings from the B_____, and this is

where they meet with Christ in particular.

Exam practice

Now answer the following exam question.

Explain **two** contrasting ways of understandings the Eucharist.   **[4 marks]**

_____

_____

_____

_____

_____

_____

_____

_____

_____

_____

Activity 4.15: Prayers in the Mass and adoration   S B   pages 112–113

Mark the following statements about prayers in the Mass and adoration as true or false.

	True	False
'The Real Presence' refers to the belief that Christ is truly present in the Eucharist.	☐	☐
Catholics believe the bread and wine become the Body and Blood during the words of adoration.	☐	☐
Taking the Bread and Wine means Catholics can share in the positive effects of Jesus' death and resurrection.	☐	☐
Agnus Dei means 'praise God'.	☐	☐
The *Agnus Dei* recalls when John the Baptist called Jesus 'the Lamb of God who takes away the sin of the world' (John 1:29, NRSV).	☐	☐
Catholics call the consecrated Bread and Wine the Blessed Sacrament.	☐	☐
In the Benediction, a consecrated host is put on display in a baptismal font.	☐	☐

Key Terms Glossary

As you progress through the course, you can collect the meanings of key terms in the glossary below. You can then use the completed glossaries to revise from.

To do well in the exam you will need to understand these terms and include them in your answers. Tick the shaded

circles to record how confident you feel. Use the extra boxes at the end to record any other terms that you have found difficult, along with their definitions.

○ **I recognise this term**

◐ **I understand what this term means**

● **I can use this term in a sentence**

Agnus Dei _____

Altar _____

Architecture _____

Artefact _____

Ascension _____

Body of Christ _____

Catechism of the Catholic Church _____

Church _____

Conscience _____

Cross _____

Crucifix _____

Eucharistic adoration

Redeemed

Lectern

Redemption

Mass

Restoration

Paschal

Resurrection

Real Presence

Risen Christ

Recreation

Sacrifice

Salvation

St Anselm

St Irenaeus

Tabernacle

Words of Institution

Chapter 5: **Church and the Kingdom of God**

A Fill in the gaps in the text below about the different places of Catholic pilgrimage.

Draw your own image of the place	Why is it important?
Jerusalem	The city in Israel where J_esus christ_ died. ✓ Catholics might visit the t_emple tomb_ ✗ where Jesus was buried, and other places connected to his life. Catholics feel closer to Jesus and renew their f_aith_ in him. ✓
Rome	A city in Italy which is the centre of the C_atholic_ faith. Contains the Vatican where the P_ope Fransic_ lives, and the tomb of St P_eter_ (the leader of the apostles). ✗ Catholics visit to show commitment to the C_atholic_ Church.
Lourdes	A town in F_rance_ where a girl called Bernadette saw visions of M_ary_, who told her to dig in the ground and a spring appeared. ✓ The w_ater_ from the spring is said to have h_ealing_ ✗ powers, so Catholics visit to bathe in the water and feel better.
Walsingham	A village in Norfolk which contains the Catholic national s_hrine_ for England. ✓ In 1061, a woman had visions of Mary's house in N_azraites_ ✗. She built a copy of it in Walsingham. This is called the Holy H_ouse_. Catholics walk between the Holy House and the S_acret_ Chapel. ✓ Allows Catholics to go on pilgrimage without having to travel abroad to another c_ountry_. ✓

B Now in the space provided in the table, draw a simple image or symbol to represent each of the four places, to help you remember why they are important.

Activity 5.2: Why go on pilgrimage?

 pages 116–119

Should Catholics go on pilgrimage? Some different opinions about this are given below.
For each opinion, try to think of a counter-argument (what someone might say to argue against it).
For example, if an opinion gives a benefit of going on pilgrimage, provide a counter-argument for why you don't need to travel to get the same benefit.

One example has been done for you.

For pilgrimage	**Against pilgrimage**
On a pilgrimage you can meet people from different places and cultures, and learn something new from them.	You don't have to travel to meet other Catholics – you can meet them at your local church.
On a pilgrimage to Rome you can renew your commitment to the Catholic Church.	*Because you can't get distract in Rome which will not allow to focus on your pilgrimage*
On a pilgrimage to Jerusalem you can visit the places Jesus lived and taught, and so feel closer to him.	*You don't need to go to place where Jesus lived & went Gods omnipresent*
Going to pilgrimage can help to be closer to God	A pilgrimage is just like going on holiday.
A pilgrimage gives you time to really think about your faith.	*You don't need to somewhere expensive you can think at home*

Exam practice

Use the activities above to help you complete the following exam question.

Give **two** reasons why Catholics go on pilgrimage. **[2 marks]**

1 *Catholic go on pilgrimage to feel closer to God or Jesus*

2 *Catholic go on pilgrimage to commited to Church again or t a or to heal*

Activity 5.3: Mission and evangelism in drama

 pages 120–121

A Read this text about mission and evangelism in drama.

A **mission** is a calling to spread the faith. The Catholic Church has a mission to take the message of Jesus to all people. Catholics take part in this mission by doing good actions and telling others about the faith. Using actions and words to spread the faith is called **evangelism**.

Drama is a good way of demonstrating mission and evangelism through the words and actions of characters. The Catholic Church says: 'The production and showing of films that have value ought to be encouraged and assured by every effective means' (*Inter Mirifica* 14).

> TIP
>
> This quotation shows that the Catholic Church approves of films that share Christian values.

B Now answer these questions about mission and evangelism in sentences.

1. Write your own definition of mission:

_____

_____

2. Write your own definition of evangelism:

_____

_____

3. Why do you think the Catholic Church encourages films that 'have value', such as films that share Christian beliefs like 'love one another'? One reason has been given below. Try to think of two more.

- *These films can inspire Christians to try to do more good in their own lives.*

- _____

  _____

- _____

  _____

Activity 5.4: The Kingdom of God and the Lord's Prayer

 page 122

The Kingdom of God refers to the idea of all people living as God intends, under his rule and authority. Creating the Kingdom of God is a gradual process.

Put these four statements about the Kingdom of God into the correct order (the **bold** words may help you).

☐ The Kingdom was **established** through Jesus' resurrection and the arrival of the Holy Spirit.

☐ The Kingdom will be **completed** at the end of time when all people will be in heaven.

☐ The Kingdom **began** when God's power came to earth in the form of Jesus.

☐ The Kingdom is **extended** by Christians who spread it among other people.

Exam practice

Now answer the following exam question.

Which **one** of the following events started the Kingdom of God?   **[1 mark]**

Put a tick (✔) in the box next to the correct answer.

A When Moses received the Ten Commandments.   ☐

B When Jesus was born.   ☐

C When Jesus died.   ☐

D When the first Pope was chosen.   ☐

Activity 5.5: The Lord's Prayer   pages 122–123

Fill in the table below and on page 88 to explain what each line of the Lord's Prayer (Matthew 6:9–13, RSV-CE) means. Try to link your explanation to the Kingdom of God where possible. One line has already been done for you.

Line from the Lord's Prayer	What I think this means
Our Father, who art in heaven	
Hallowed be thy name	*This line is asking for people to view God's name as being very special and holy. When people view God in this way, they will become part of God's kingdom.*
Thy kingdom come	
Thy will be done, on earth as it is in heaven	
Give us this day our daily bread	
And forgive us our trespasses as we forgive those who trespass against us	

And lead us not into temptation	
But deliver us from evil	

Activity 5.6: Justice, peace and reconciliation

 pages 124–125

The statements below have been muddled up. They describe some of the ways that Catholics can help the Kingdom of God to grow. Copy each statement into the correct box, depending on whether you think they help to create justice, peace or reconciliation.

- Helping people to work together by learning from the past.
- Bringing about what is right and fair according to the law.
- Removing violence and conflict.
- Restoring relationships between people.
- Creating a state of trust and unity between people.
- Making sure people have access to basic human rights.

Justice:

Peace:

Reconciliation:

Activity 5.7: The Second Vatican Council

 pages 126–127

A Read this text about the Second Vatican Council.

Sometimes the Pope will consult other members of the Catholic Church to help him make a decision. In the 1960s, the Pope called the bishops together at the Second Vatican Council to decide how to make the Church more open and accessible. They produced four major documents:

<table>
<tr>
<td>

***Dei Verbum* (The Word of God)**

- Deals with the importance and interpretation of the Bible.

- Stresses that the Bible is important but should not be taken in a literal way.

</td>
<td>

***Sacrosanctum Concilium* (On the Sacred Liturgy)**

- Deals with church services.

- Emphasises that people should have a full part in worship.

- Allows the Mass to be celebrated in a country's own language, not just in Latin.

</td>
</tr>
<tr>
<td>

***Lumen Gentium* (On the Church)**

- Deals with the nature and structure of the Church.

- Stresses that all Catholics have an important role to play.

- Emphasises the idea of a pilgrim Church moving forwards within the modern world.

</td>
<td>

***Gaudium et Spes* (The Church in the Modern World)**

- Deals with issues in modern society.

- Stresses that the Church should not be separate from society, but that it should guide people on how they live.

</td>
</tr>
</table>

B Now answer the following questions about the Second Vatican Council.

1. What was the purpose of the Second Vatican Council?

_____

_____

2. Which members of the Church took part in the Second Vatican Council?

_____

3. What change did the Second Vatican Council make to the Mass?

_____

_____

4. Which document said that the Bible should not be interpreted literally?

_____

5. Did the Second Vatican Council stress that the Church should be a part of modern society or separate from it?

_____

6. Which document talked about the structure of the Church?

_____

Exam practice

Now answer the following exam question.

Explain **two** contrasting views about whether changes made at the Second Vatican Council are likely to have helped the Catholic Church in today's world. **[4 marks]**

_____

_____

_____

_____

_____

_____

_____

_____

_____

_____

Activity 5.8: Mary and the Magnificat

SB pages 128–129

Fill in the gaps in the following sentences about the Magnificat using some of the words provided. (There are more words than gaps – you will have to decide which ones to leave out.)

blessed	Elizabeth	patience	prayer	God	Emily
creed	need	lost	trusted	Mary	rich
Son	Jesus	praise	poor	greatness	

	The Magnificat
Who?	Spoken by _____ when she visited her cousin _____ after she had been told that she was going to have a baby (J_____).
What?	The Magnificat is a _____ in which Mary praised God for his _____ and for choosing her to give birth to his _____. She felt truly _____ and made it clear that she was very happy to accept the role that _____ had given her.

Why?	Mary wanted to _____ God and show that she _____
	God to make everything work out well. She also highlighted the belief that God will look after the
	_____ and those in _____ .

Sources of religious belief and teaching

SB page 128

Learn some short quotations from the Magnificat.

A

❝My soul magnifies the Lord❞
Luke 1:46, NRSV

In this quotation Mary is praising God.

Fill in the gaps below. It will help you to learn the quotation if you say the whole thing out loud every time you write it.

❝My _____ magnifies the _____❞

Now cover up the text above and have a go at writing out the whole quotation from memory.

❝_____❞

B

❝he has filled the hungry with good things, and sent the rich away empty.❞
Luke 1:53, NRSV

This quotation shows that Mary believes God will help the poor and those in need.

TIP

Some people think the Magnificat is controversial because it could encourage the poor to rebel against the rich and powerful in order to spread the Kingdom of God.

Fill in the gaps below. It will help you to learn the quotation if you say the whole thing out loud every time you write it.

❝he has _____ the hungry with _____

things and _____ the rich _____ empty.❞

❝he has _____ the _____ with good

_____ and _____ the _____ away

_____.❞

Now cover up the text above and have a go at writing out the whole quotation from memory.

❝_____❞

Exam practice

Now answer the following exam question.

Explain **two** beliefs about God that are shown in the Magnificat.

Refer to scripture or another source of Christian belief and teaching in your answer.

[5 marks]

_____

_____

_____

_____

_____

_____

_____

_____

_____

_____

_____

_____

_____

> **TIP**
> You can use your answers to Activity 5.12 and one or two of the quotations you have just learned to answer the exam question.

Key terms

pages 130–131

A There are four qualities or 'marks' that define the nature of the Catholic Church. These qualities and their meanings have been muddled up. Write out the meanings in the correct order in the second table below.

One	The beliefs of the Church are universal
Holy	The Church's teachings are built on the teachings of the 12 apostles
Catholic	The Church is one united body
Apostolic	The presence of God makes the Church holy

One	
Holy	

Catholic	
Apostolic	

B Now write the correct term beside each meaning. For an extra challenge, cover up the rest of this activity and try to see if you can recall the words from memory.

The beliefs of the Church are universal	
The Church's teachings are built on the teachings of the 12 apostles	
The Church is one united body	
The presence of God makes the Church holy	

Activity 5.9: Apostolic succession and the Magisterium

pages 131

The apostles were Jesus' original followers. 'Apostolic succession' is the idea that the Pope and bishops are the successors to these apostles: they inherit their responsibilities.

A Some beliefs about apostolic succession and the Magisterium are given below. Fill in the gaps in the sentences.

The P_____ and bishops are successors to the a_____ .	The a_____ of the apostles has been passed down through the generations.
The authority of P_____ (who led the apostles) is passed down to successive P_____ (who lead the Church today).	The combined authority of the Pope and the bishops is known as the M_____ .
The Church is guided by the H_____ S_____ .	When the Pope speaks about doctrine, his word is i_____ – it cannot be wrong.

B Now in each box draw a symbol or picture to help you remember what it means.

Activity 5.10: The Church as conciliar and pontifical

 pages 132–133

The Church is **conciliar** because it makes important decisions through council meetings. It is also **pontifical** because it is led by the Pope, who has the highest authority.

These statements have been muddled up. Copy them into the correct column of the table below based on whether you think they are about the Church being conciliar or pontifical.

- The Pope is the successor to St Peter.

- Some decisions are made at Councils (meetings of the Pope and bishops).

- Allows the Pope to discuss difficult decisions with others.

- The Pope is God's representative on earth.

- The Second Vatican Council is an example.

- Means that different people's views are represented.

- All Council decisions have to be approved by the Pope.

- Means the bishops (who are the successors to the apostles) can be involved in decision-making.

- The Pope's teachings are infallible (without error).

Conciliar	Pontifical

Exam practice

Using your answers to Activities 5.9 and 5.10, answer the following exam question.

'It is best for the Church to have one special person as God's representative to make all decisions.'

Evaluate this statement. In your answer you should:

- give reasoned arguments to support this statement
- give reasoned arguments to support a different point of view
- refer to Christian teaching
- reach a justified conclusion.

[12 marks]
[+3 SPaG marks]

 REMEMBER...

Focus your answer on the statement you are asked to evaluate.

- Try to write at least three paragraphs – one with arguments to support the statement, one with arguments to support a different point of view, and a final paragraph with a justified conclusion stating which side you think is more convincing, and why.
- Look at the bullet points in the question, and make sure you include everything that they ask for.
- The key skill that you need to demonstrate is evaluation. This means expressing judgements on the arguments that support or oppose the statement, based on evidence. You might decide an argument is strong because it is based on a source of religious belief and teaching, such as a teaching from the Bible, or because it is based on scientific evidence. You might decide an argument is weak because it is based on a personal opinion, or a popular idea with no scientific basis. You can use phrases in your chains of reasoning such as 'I think this a convincing argument because…' or 'In my opinion, this is a weak argument because…'.

Activity 5.11: Catholic social teaching

S B page 133

A Read the following text about Catholic social teaching.

Below are five reasons why it is important to help others.

- Jesus helped others.
- God loves all people.
- Helping others makes yourself feel good.
- It is important to reduce inequality and suffering in society.
- Helping others is a way to spread the Kingdom of God.

B Now answer these questions about Catholic social teaching in sentences.

1. Which reason do you think is most important to the Catholic Church from the list above?

_____

2. Why do you think this is the most important reason?

_____

_____

_____

TIP

There is no correct answer as such here – what is more important is that you can explain your choice and provide evidence to back it up.

3. Is there any evidence you can use to support your choice? For example, Catholic teachings or quotations from the Bible? Write your evidence down here.

_____

_____

_____

Sources of religious belief and teaching

S B page 134

Learn the following quotation about God's commandment to love.

❝You shall love your neighbour as yourself.❞
Mark 12:31, NRSV

This quotation shows that Christians are called to show love by treating others as well as they would want to be treated.

Fill in the gaps below. It will help you to learn the quotation if you say the whole thing out loud every time you write it.

❝You _____ love your _____ as _____.❞

Now cover up the text above and have a go at writing out the whole quotation from memory.

❝_____❞

Activity 5.12: SVP and CAFOD pages 134–135

A Read the following text about the SVP and CAFOD.

SVP (St Vincent de Paul Society)	CAFOD (Catholic Agency for Overseas Development)
• Works in small groups to help people in a local area. • Members visit people in need in their homes, or in hospitals and prisons. • They may do practical things like shopping and household chores. • SVP also run larger community projects, such as summer camps for children.	• Works at a national and global level to help people in other countries and to try to bring about large-scale change. • Provides emergency aid in response to natural disasters or war. • Supplies long-term aid such as irrigation, education and healthcare. • Challenges national and international policies and laws that harm the poor or the environment.

B Tick the correct box below to show whether each statement is about SVP or CAFOD, or both.

	SVP	CAFOD	Both
An example of a Catholic charity that works nationally and globally.	☐	☐	☐
An example of a Catholic charity that works locally.	☐	☐	☐
Campaigns against national laws that harm those living in poverty.	☐	☐	☐
Provides help to victims of war.	☐	☐	☐
Provides practical help to people in the local area.	☐	☐	☐
Provides aid that helps in the long-term, such as farming equipment.	☐	☐	☐
Runs local community projects.	☐	☐	☐

C Now answer the following questions.

1. In your own words, write a short summary of two or three sentences to describe SVP and the work it does.

_____

_____

_____

_____

_____

2. In your own words, write a short summary of two or three sentences to describe CAFOD and the work it does.

_____

_____

_____

_____

_____

Activity 5.13: Christian vocations

pages 136–137

Fill in the gaps in the sentences below about different Christian vocations.

Priesthood	A p_____ is an ordained minister in the Catholic Church. He is chosen to celebrate M_____, preach and f_____ sins. Priests do not marry or have sex because they are committed fully to G_____. This is called c_____. Priests serve others, just like J_____ did, and promise to obey the b_____ whose diocese their church is in. In this way they are obeying G_____.
Family life	L_____ is the Kingdom value that keeps a family together. Catholic parents try to show K_____ values to others in their family. In teaching their c_____ Kingdom values, they help to spread the Kingdom of God on earth.
Religious life	Monks and n_____ commit themselves totally to God by living in a small community which focuses on p_____ and worship. They take vows of p_____, chastity and o_____ to God. Religious brothers and s_____ focus on God in a similar way but spend a lot of time in the local c_____ helping others. They take on caring roles such as nursing and teaching to show l_____ through helping others.

Activity 5.14: Kingdom values in the life of a Catholic pages 138–139

A Here are five definitions. Choose the best definition for each of the three terms below, then write it out beside each term.

- Restoring harmony after relationships have broken down.

- Passing the authority of the apostles on to the bishops.

- A state of total trust and unity between people.

- Bringing about what is right and fair; creating equality among people.

- Receiving freedom from the power of sin.

Justice: _____

_____

Peace: _____

_____

Reconciliation: _____

_____

B All of the statements below are about Pope Francis and the ways he shows the Kingdom values of justice, peace and reconciliation in his own life. Decide whether you think each statement is about justice, peace or reconciliation, and write your choice in the space after each one. One has already been done for you.

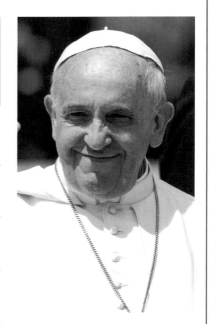

He doesn't allow money to be wasted on himself and lives in a small flat. _____*justice*_____

He has visited areas of tension in the world, trying to end conflict. _____

During 2014–15, he helped to restore relations between the USA and Cuba. _____

He has criticised economic policies that lead to inequality. _____

He has broken down barriers between Catholics, Jews and Muslims. _____

As a bishop, he increased the number of priests working with the poor. _____

Key Terms Glossary

As you progress through the course, you can collect the meanings of key terms in the glossary below. You can then use the completed glossaries to revise from.

To do well in the exam you will need to understand these terms and include them in your answers. Tick the shaded circles to record how confident you feel. Use the extra boxes at the end to record any other terms that you have found difficult, along with their definitions.

○ **I recognise this term**

◔ **I understand what this term means**

● **I can use this term in a sentence**

Apostolic _____

_____

_____

_____

_____

Apostolic succession _____

_____

_____

_____

_____

Catholic _____

_____

_____

_____

_____

Conciliar _____

_____

_____

_____

_____

Discipleship _____

_____

_____

_____

_____

Dramatised prayer _____

_____

_____

_____

_____

Four marks of the Church _____

_____

_____

_____

_____

Hierarchy _____

_____

_____

_____

_____

Holy _____

_____

_____

_____

_____

Holy sites _____

_____

_____

_____

_____

Jerusalem _____

_____

_____

_____

_____

Justice _____
_____
_____
_____
_____

Mary _____
_____
_____
_____
_____

Kingdom of God (Reign of God) _____
_____
_____
_____
_____

Peace _____
_____
_____
_____
_____

Kingdom values _____
_____
_____
_____
_____

Pilgrimage _____
_____
_____
_____
_____

Lourdes _____
_____
_____
_____
_____

Pontifical _____
_____
_____
_____
_____

Lumen Gentium _____
_____
_____
_____
_____

Priesthood _____
_____
_____
_____
_____

Magnificat _____
_____
_____
_____
_____

Rome _____
_____
_____
_____
_____

Sacrosanctum Concilium

Stations of the Cross

The Lord's Prayer

Vocation

Walsingham

Chapter 6: **Eschatology**

Fill in the gaps in the sentences below about the Paschal candle.

The Paschal candle represents the

R_____

C_____ .

The five grains of i_____

represent the five wounds that

C_____ received during

his c_____ .

At the Easter Vigil, everyone is given a

c_____ lit from the Paschal

candle, to show that all believers share in the

risen glory of C_____ .

The A_____ and

O_____ symbols

show that Christ is eternal.

During a b_____ ,

the person being baptised is given a candle

lit from the P_____

candle. This shows they have been filled with

the l_____ of Christ.

During the Easter V_____ , the

priest lights the Paschal candle from a fire. This represents

the l_____ of Christ overcoming

s_____ and death.

Exam practice

Now answer the following exam question.

Give **two** ways the Paschal Candle is used by Catholics.   **[2 marks]**

1 _____

_____

2 _____

_____

Activity 6.2: Michelangelo's *The Last Judgement*

 pages 144–145

This painting by Michelangelo shows the Last Judgement. Answer the questions about it below in sentences.

1. What do Christians believe will happen at the Last Judgement?

   _____

   _____

   _____

   _____

   _____

2. Why is Christ's right hand raised in the centre of the painting ❶ ?

   _____

   _____

   _____

   _____

   _____

3. The saints are shown as having perfect bodies, despite having been tortured and killed ❷ . Why is this?

   _____

   _____

   _____

4. Hell is a place where the light of Christ can't reach people who have rejected God. How is this shown in the painting ❸ ?

   _____

   _____

   _____

5. One of the angels is holding a small book filled with the names of those who will be raised to heaven. Another angel is holding a larger book filled with the names of those going to hell ❹ . What does this show? Tick the correct answer.

   ☐ That everyone will be raised to heaven.

   ☐ That people need to do good and follow Jesus' teachings, because they can't assume they will go to heaven.

   ☐ That it has already been determined if someone goes to heaven or hell before they are born.

Key terms

pages 136–143

A These terms and their meanings are muddled up. Write out the meanings in the correct order in the second table below.

Tombstone	Something built to remember an important person
Remembrance garden	A large carved stone placed over a person's grave
Monument	An outside area where the ashes of cremated people can be buried

Tombstone	
Remembrance garden	
Monument	

B Now write the correct term beside each meaning. For an extra challenge, cover up the rest of this activity and try to see if you can recall the words from memory.

An outside area where the ashes of cremated people can be buried	
Something built to remember an important person	
A large carved stone placed over a person's grave	

Activity 6.3: Eschatology and life after death

pages 148–149

A Read this text about eschatology.

Eschatology is the study of what will happen at the end of time, and covers things such as death, judgement, heaven and hell. Christians can't be sure what will happen because it is something only God knows, and Jesus is the only person who has been able to give some idea of what happens after death.

In the Bible, Mark's Gospel predicts that at the end of time, there will be cosmic disasters such as the sun darkening and the stars falling out of the skies. Christ will then judge the whole of creation, and God will reign in glory (Mark 13:24–27, NRSV).

Christians believe Jesus' resurrection teaches that life continues after death in the presence of God.

TIP

You can use Mark's predictions about what will happen at the end of time to help answer questions on eschatology. These predictions can act as a source of Christian belief and teaching for the 5-mark question.

B Now answer the following questions in your own words.

1. What is eschatology?

_____

_____

2. Why are Christians not sure what will happen at the end of time?

_____

_____

_____

3. In the Bible, what does Mark predict will happen at the end of time?

_____

_____

_____

4. What does Jesus' resurrection teach Christians about what happens when they die?

_____

_____

_____

Activity 6.4: Paul's letter on resurrection

page 149

A Read the following text about Paul's letter on resurrection.

Some Christians believe that when they die, they will be resurrected in some way. In the Bible, Paul writes about the differences between a person's earthly body and their resurrected body:

> **"** So it is with the resurrection of the dead. What is sown is perishable, what is raised is imperishable. It is sown in dishonour, it is raised in glory. It is sown in weakness, it is raised in power. It is sown a physical body, it is raised a spiritual body. If there is a physical body, there is also a spiritual body. **"**
>
> *1 Corinthians* 15:42–44, NRSV

TIP

You can refer to this quotation in your exam when writing about what Christians believe happens after death. This quotation shows that some Christians think people will have resurrected bodies in heaven.

B Mark the following statements about Paul's writings on resurrection as true or false.

	True	False
People are not resurrected from the dead.	☐	☐
A resurrected body will be powerful and strong.	☐	☐
A resurrected body will be sinless and perfect.	☐	☐
A resurrected body will eventually decay and fade away.	☐	☐
There is no difference between a person's resurrected body and their earthly body.	☐	☐

c For all the statements you have marked as 'false', write one or two sentences with the correct information. One example has been completed for you.

People are resurrected from the dead. Paul writes that physical bodies are raised as spiritual bodies, i.e. they are resurrected.

_____

_____

_____

_____

Activity 6.5: The four last things

pages 150–151

A Fill in the gaps in the sentences using the words provided. You should use every word once.

will	body	responsibility	angry	heaven	life
love	merciful	accept	hell	reunited	soul
separation	happiness	judges	God		

Death

- Death is a change to a new phase of _____ .

- The _____ lives on but the _____ dies.

- The soul is judged by _____ and goes to heaven, hell or Purgatory.

- At the end of time, the body and soul will be _____ .

Judgement

- God _____ a person after their death, considering all they have done.

- People have to accept _____ for their actions.

- God's judgement will be _____ because Jesus died so all could be saved.

Heaven

- People who are judged favourably enter _____ .

- This is the state of eternal _____ in the presence of God.

- God's _____ removes all cares and worries.

- People have to use their free _____ to choose to accept God in order to enter heaven.

Hell

- People who are judged unfavourably enter _____ .

- This is the state of eternal _____ from God.

- People choose hell for themselves because they do not _____ God.

- People in hell realise what they have thrown away and so are _____

  with themselves.

B In each box, draw a picture or symbol to represent death, judgement, heaven and hell.

Exam practice

Now answer the following exam question.

Explain **two** Christian beliefs about heaven.

Refer to scripture or another source of Christian belief and teaching in your answer.　　　**[5 marks]**

_____

_____

_____

_____

_____

_____

_____

_____

_____

_____

_____

_____

_____

_____

Activity 6.6: Purgatory and judgement

 pages 152–153

Using the definitions below to help you, decide whether the following statements are about purgatory, particular judgement or final judgement. Write your answers on the lines provided. One has been done for you.

- **Purgatory:** a process of cleansing to remove the effects of sin, and to help a person accept the full presence of God

- **Particular judgement:** when a person is judged by God after they die

- **Final judgement:** when Christ returns at the end of time to judge the whole of creation

Happens immediately after a person dies. _____Particular judgement_____

A process that allows a person to make up for wrong actions. _____

Results in a person going to heaven, hell or purgatory. _____

Happens at the end of time. _____

Prayers from those still alive may help the process. _____

When Christ will come in glory to judge everything. _____

After this, the reign of God will be established. _____

People go here because of bad things they did. _____

When a person is judged personally on all their actions. _____

Activity 6.7: Different Christian beliefs about the afterlife

page 153

Because nobody really knows what happens when a person dies, not all Christian denominations agree about what happens in the afterlife.

Copy out the correct belief for each group in the boxes below.

- Do not believe in Purgatory. They believe that after judgement, all will either go straight to heaven by accepting God, or to hell by rejecting God.

- Believe that people wait in their graves for the second coming of Christ when they will be judged and sent to heaven or hell.

- Believe in resurrection and heaven.

All Christians…	Many Christians…	Some Christians…

Exam practice

Use your answers to Activities 6.6 and 6.7 to answer the following question.

'All Christians will go to heaven straight away when they die.'

Evaluate this statement. In your answer you should:

- give reasoned arguments to support this statement
- give reasoned arguments to support a different point of view
- refer to Christian teaching
- reach a justified conclusion.

[12 marks]
[+3 SPaG marks]

 REMEMBER...

Focus your answer on the statement you are asked to evaluate.

- Try to write at least three paragraphs – one with arguments to support the statement, one with arguments to support a different point of view, and a final paragraph with a justified conclusion stating which side you think is more convincing, and why.

- Look at the bullet points in the question, and make sure you include everything that they ask for.

- The key skill that you need to demonstrate is evaluation. This means expressing judgements on the arguments that support or oppose the statement, based on evidence. You might decide an argument is strong because it is based on a source of religious belief and teaching, such as a teaching from the Bible, or because it is based on scientific evidence. You might decide an argument is weak because it is based on a personal opinion, or a popular idea with no scientific basis. You can use phrases in your chains of reasoning such as 'I think this a convincing argument because...' or 'In my opinion, this is a weak argument because...'.

Activity 6.8: The parable of the Rich Man and Lazarus

 pages 154–155

A The following boxes describe the different things that happen in the Parable of the Rich Man and Lazarus (Luke 16:19–31), but they are muddled up. Number the boxes from 1 to 6 to show what order they should go in, with '1' being the first thing that happens in the parable and '6' being the last event.

○ The rich man then asks Abraham to warn his brothers about how bad hell is.

○ In hell, the rich man suffers. He asks for help from Abraham to ease his suffering, but Abraham refuses.

○ A rich man doesn't share any of his food with the poor, homeless man called Lazarus who lives outside his house.

○ Abraham points out to the rich man that it is not possible to travel between heaven and hell.

○ Abraham refuses and says that his brothers should listen to the prophets. If they don't have faith in God then Abraham's warning will make no difference.

○ Lazarus dies and is taken to heaven to be with Abraham. The rich man dies and goes to hell.

TIP

As this parable was written in the Bible nearly 2,000 years ago, the image it paints of heaven and hell should not be taken literally. Its religious message is still relevant though.

B Now answer the following questions.

1. Explain two things that the parable teaches about heaven and hell.

1 _____

_____

_____

2 _____

_____

_____

2. What message does the parable give about how people should live their lives on earth?

_____

_____

_____

_____

_____

Sources of religious belief and teaching

SB · pages 156–157

Learn the quotations below about cosmic reconciliation.

A

❝through him God was pleased to reconcile to himself all things, whether on earth or in heaven, by making peace through the blood of his cross.❞
Colossians 1:20, NRSV

This quotation from **St Paul** shows that Jesus' death helped to start the process of cosmic reconciliation.

Fill in the gaps below. It will help you to learn the quotation if you say the whole thing out loud every time you write it.

❝through him _____ was pleased to _____ to

himself all _____ , whether on _____ or in heaven,

by making _____ through the blood of his _____ .❞

Now cover up the text above and have a go at writing out the whole quotation from memory.

❝_____

_____

_____

_____❞

B

❝all shall be well❞
Revelations of Divine Love 32

This is something that Jesus said to **Julian of Norwich**, when he appeared to her in a vision. Jesus is saying that everything will be 'well' because everything will be made perfect at the end of time. The whole of creation will be reconciled with God.

Fill in the gaps below to help you learn this second quotation.

❝all _____ be _____❞

Now cover up the text above and have a go at writing out the whole quotation from memory.

❝_____❞

TIP

'Cosmic reconciliation' is a difficult term but try to remember what it means. You can think of it like this:

Reconciling (bringing together in harmony) the **cosmos** (the whole of creation) with **God**.

Christians believe this will happen at the end of time.

Activity 6.9: The Church's teachings on the end of time

 pages 158–159

A The first column of the table below outlines Catholic beliefs about the end of time.
Fill in the second column to explain how these beliefs influence the way that Catholics live their lives today. Use a teaching from the list which directs the decisions Catholics should make. One example has been completed for you.

TIP 'Predestined' means that something has already been decided before a person is born. Christians believe people choose themselves whether to go to heaven or hell – this has not already been decided for them.

Belief	How this belief influences the way that Catholics live their lives, including a relevant teaching
At the end of time, Christ will come in glory as the judge and saviour.	Catholics live their lives in the hope this will happen: 'There will come the time of the restoration of all things' (Lumen Gentium 48). Catholics try to spread Jesus' teachings to help build the Kingdom of God.
No one is predestined to go to heaven or hell.	
People send themselves to hell by choosing to reject God.	
No one knows when the end of time will happen.	

Teachings:

❝We may merit to enter into the marriage feast with him and to be numbered among the blessed.❞

(*Lumen Gentium* 48 – Vatican II)

❝There will come the time of the restoration of all things.❞

(*Lumen Gentium* 48 – Vatican II)

❝For this (hell), a wilful turning away from God (a mortal sin) is necessary.❞

(*Catechism of the Catholic Church* 1037)

❝Since however we know not the day nor the hour, on Our Lords advice we must be constantly vigilant.❞

(*Lumen Gentium* 48 – Vatican II)

❝God predestines no one to go to hell.❞

(*Catechism of the Catholic Church* 1037)

B Now answer the following question.

What do you think is the most important thing that Catholics should do to try to earn a place in heaven? Give reasons for your answer.

_____
_____
_____
_____
_____
_____
_____
_____
_____
_____

Exam practice

Now answer the following exam question.

Explain **two** ways in which teachings on the end of time may influence the way Christians live their lives.

[4 marks]

_____
_____
_____
_____
_____
_____
_____
_____
_____
_____

Activity 6.10: The anointing of the sick

 pages 160–161

The statements below are muddled up. Copy them out into the correct places in the table below to show the meanings of the different actions used in the anointing of the sick.

- Through the anointing, the person is given hope of a new life, either healed in this life or in eternal happiness with God.

- This is a reminder of baptism.

- Taking the bread and wine shows that Christ will support the sick person.

- This helps the sick person to face the future with a clear conscience.

- The Holy Spirit gives the person strength and a sense of peace.

Action	Meaning
The priest sprinkles the sick person with holy water.	
The priest lays his hands on the head of the sick person and calls down the Holy Spirit.	
The priest anoints the forehead and hands of the sick person with oil.	
The sick person confesses their sins and receives forgiveness from the priest.	
The sick person receives Holy Communion from the priest.	

Activity 6.11: Commendation of the dying

 page 161

A The statements below are muddled up. Copy them out into the correct places in the table below, to match the different actions used in the commendation of the dying with their meanings.

- The dying person receives their last Holy Communion.

- A prayer may be said that includes the words 'May you live in peace this day, may your home be with God in Zion'.

- The dying person may hold a crucifix.

- A Litany of the Saints is said.

- A short passage from the Bible may be read.

Action	Meaning
	This reminds the dying person that they are sharing in Christ's death.
	This reading reassures the person that God is with them.
	Saints are asked to pray for the dying person before they face God's judgement.
	This shows the dying person that Christ is with them on their journey to a new life.
	Expresses the hope that the dying person will soon be in eternal peace and happiness with God in heaven.

B Now answer the following question.

1. How do you think the commendation of the dying helps the dying person and their family? Explain your reasoning.

_____

_____

_____

_____

_____

_____

Activity 6.12: The funeral rite

(S B) pages 162–163

A Mark the following statements about the funeral rite as true or false.

	True	False
Taking the coffin to church represents the deceased person being taken back to God.	☐	☐
The coffin is placed beside the tabernacle.	☐	☐
The readings of the Mass focus on the effects of Christ's resurrection.	☐	☐
Smoke from burning incense is waved over the coffin.	☐	☐
Sprinkling holy water over the coffin is a reminder of the person's ordination.	☐	☐
At the burial, prayers express the hope that the deceased person is waiting for God's judgement.	☐	☐

B For all the statements you have marked as 'false', write one or two sentences with the correct information.

_____

_____

_____

_____

_____

_____

_____

_____

Activity 6.13: The sanctity of life and euthanasia   pages 164–165

A Read the text below about the sanctity of life and euthanasia.

'Sanctity of life' is the idea that all human life is holy and sacred because God created it. This means that all life should be respected and valued. This includes the lives of the ill and elderly, who should be cared for with dignity.

'Euthanasia' means intentionally helping someone to die in order to end their suffering. The Catholic Church is against euthanasia for a number of reasons, one of which is that it goes against the sanctity of life.

B Now answer the following questions in your own words.

> TIP
>
> The sanctity of life is a key Christian teaching that you can talk about when answering questions on life and death, such as questions about euthanasia or abortion.

1. What does 'sanctity of life' mean?

_____

_____

2. How does the sanctity of life apply to people who are elderly or very ill?

_____

3. What does 'euthanasia' mean?

_____

4. One reason is given below for why the Catholic Church is against euthanasia. Add two more reasons.

1 _Medication can help to reduce a person's suffering._ _____

2 _____

3 _____

Exam practice

Now answer the following exam question.

Which **one** of the following is the meaning of euthanasia?   **[1 mark]**

Put a tick (✔) in the box next to the correct answer.

A Deliberately ending a person's life to relieve suffering.   ☐

B Eternal life in heaven with God.   ☐

C Life is sacred and holy because it was created by God.   ☐

D The first part of the funeral rite.   ☐

Key Terms Glossary

As you progress through the course, you can collect the meanings of key terms in the glossary below. You can then use the completed glossaries to revise from.

To do well in the exam you will need to understand these terms and include them in your answers. Tick the shaded

circles to record how confident you feel. Use the extra boxes at the end to record any other terms that you have found difficult, along with their definitions.

- ○ **I recognise this term**
- ◐ **I understand what this term means**
- ● **I can use this term in a sentence**

Cosmic reconciliation

Eschatology

Eternity

Euthanasia

Final judgement

Funeral rites

Michelangelo's *Last Judgement*

Monuments

Mother Julian of Norwich

Particular judgement

Paschal candle

Prayers

Purgatory

Remembrance garden

The last rites

The Rich Man and Lazarus

Tombstones

Chapter 7: **Exam practice**

Test the 1-mark question

Example

1 Which **one** of the following terms means that God is beyond and outside life on earth and the universe? **[1 mark]**

Put a tick (✔) in the box next to the correct answer.

A Omnipotent. ☐

B Stewardship. ☐

C Transcendent. ✔

D Magisterium. ☐ ✔ *(1)*

WHAT WILL THE QUESTION LOOK LIKE?

The 1-mark question will always be a **multiple-choice question** with four answers to choose from. Only one answer is correct. The question will usually start with the words '**Which one of the following…**'

HOW IS IT MARKED?

You will receive 1 mark for a correct response.

> **! REMEMBER…**
>
> Read the question carefully before making your choice. Even if you are not sure of the right answer, make a guess – you may get it right anyway.
>
> Be aware that if you tick more than one box, you will receive no marks, even if one of your selected answers is correct.

Activity

2 Which **one** of the following symbols is pictured as a fish? **[1 mark]**

Put a tick (✔) in the box next to the correct answer.

A Alpha. ☐

B Omega. ☐

C Ichthus. ☐

D Chi-Ro. ☐

3 Which **one** of the following is a reading stand from which the Bible readings are given? **[1 mark]**

Put a tick (✔) in the box next to the correct answer.

A Lectern. ☐

B Altar. ☐

C Crucifix. ☐

D Tabernacle. ☐

4 Which **one** of the following is not one of the four marks of the Church?   **[1 mark]**

Put a tick (✓) in the box next to the correct answer.

A One. ☐

B Apostolic. ☐

C Holy. ☐

D Justice. ☐

5 Which **one** of the following is the meaning of resurrection?   **[1 mark]**

Put a tick (✓) in the box next to the correct answer.

A Ascending to heaven. ☐

B Rising from the dead. ☐

C Dying through being fixed to a cross. ☐

D Being filled with the power of the Holy Spirit. ☐

Test the 2-mark question

Example

> **WHAT WILL THE QUESTION LOOK LIKE?**
>
> The 2-mark question will always start with the words **'Give two…'** or **'Name two…'**, and a maximum of **2 marks** will be awarded.

1 Give **two** Christian beliefs about free will.   **[2 marks]**

   1 *Christians believe that God gave humans free will.* ✓ *(1)*

   2 *Christians believe that free will is why sin exists.* ✓ *(1)*

> **HOW IS IT MARKED?**
>
> In your answer you should provide two facts or short ideas; **you don't need to explain them or express any opinions**. For each correct response you will receive 1 mark.

> (!) **REMEMBER…**
>
> You need to give **two pieces of information** in your answer. Use the numbered lines to make sure you write two separate points. Don't just repeat yourself – make each point say something new.

Activity

2 Name **two** places that Catholics go to on pilgrimage.   **[2 marks]**

> The sample answer below would get 1 mark because only one correct answer is given. Add a new place of pilgrimage to make the answer worth 2 marks.

Jerusalem

_____

3 Give **two** ways that Catholics might carry out their duty to be stewards at a local level.   **[2 marks]**

1 _____

   _____

2 _____

   _____

4 Name **two** persons of the Trinity.   **[2 marks]**

1 _____

   _____

2 _____

   _____

TIP

For 2-mark questions like this one, it is ok to write your answers as single words. You don't need to waste time writing in complete sentences.

Test the 4-mark question

Example

1 Explain **two** ways in which music influences Catholic worship. **[4 marks]**

One way in which music influences Catholic worship is that it helps to make it a more communal activity. ✓ **(1)** *The use of hymns and other types of music helps everyone to feel more involved in the worship.* ✓ **(1)**

Another way is that it can make worship feel more joyous or solemn. ✓ **(1)** *For example, an upbeat contemporary worship song can help to make a church service feel more lively.* ✓ **(1)**

WHAT WILL THE QUESTION LOOK LIKE?

The 4-mark question will always start with the words '**Explain two…**', and a maximum of **4 marks** will be awarded. You are asked to 'Explain', which means you need to show extra detail in both of your points for full marks.

HOW IS IT MARKED?

This answer would gain 4 marks because it makes two different points, and both points clearly show extra detail.

! REMEMBER…

Make **two different points**, each in a separate paragraph. Try to show the examiner clearly where each point begins. For example, start your answer with 'One way is…' and then move on to your second point by saying 'Another way is…'.

Try to add more detail to each point, by giving an example or adding more explanation. Adding detail to your points in this way will earn you more marks.

Activity

2 Explain **two** contrasting views about the sanctity of life. **[4 marks]**

The sample answer below would get 4 marks because there are two points, each with extra detail. Add a tick next to each point. Then underline the extra detail that has been added to each point.

Christians believe that God created all life and made it holy. This means that as life is a gift from God, it should be respected and everything should be done to keep it going.

Some others agree with the idea that life is sacred, but believe that God would not want life to continue if a person is suffering badly, or if they are being kept alive on a machine when they have no chance of getting better.

TIP

It is a good idea to start your second point on a new line, to make it clear where it begins.

3 Explain **two** ways in which the Parable of the Rich Man and Lazarus influences Christians today. **[4 marks]**

The sample answer below would get 2 marks because it makes one point and then adds extra detail to this point. Add a second point for a third mark. If you can add detail to that point with an appropriate example or more explanation, the complete answer will get 4 marks.

One way the parable influences Christians today is that it encourages the rich to help the poor. ✓ **(1)** *This means they would support charities such as food banks.* ✓ **(1)**

A second way… _____

_____

_____

4 Explain **two** ways that the words of the Lord's Prayer influences Christians today. **[4 marks]**

The sample answer below would get 2 marks for giving two different ways. Add detail to each point to gain 2 more marks.

One way is that Christians ask God to forgive them. ✓ *(1)*

_____

_____

_____

_____

A second way is that Christians ask for God's Kingdom to come. ✓ *(1)*

_____

_____

_____

_____

5 Explain **two** contrasting views about the incarnation. **[4 marks]**

_____

_____

_____

_____

_____

_____

_____

_____

_____

_____

6 Explain **two** ways that belief in the Trinity influences Christians today.

[4 marks]

_____

_____

_____

_____

_____

_____

_____

_____

_____

_____

Test the 5-mark question

Example

1 Explain **two** ways in which Jesus is the fulfilment of the law.

Refer to scripture or another source of Christian belief and teaching in your answer. **[5 marks]**

One way in which Jesus is the fulfilment of the law is that he always obeyed God's commands. ✓ (1) For example, he always showed love and forgiveness to other people. ✓ (1)

A second way is that Jesus developed the law to make it more perfect. ✓ (1) Jesus taught that it was more important to focus on having the right attitude than to just follow the commandments in the Old Testament. ✓ (1) For example, he listed good attitudes to have in the Beatitudes, such as 'Blessed are the merciful'. ✓ (1)

WHAT WILL THE QUESTION LOOK LIKE?

The 5-mark question will always start with the words **'Explain two…'** and end with the words **'Refer to scripture or another source of Christian belief and teaching in your answer'**. A maximum of **5 marks** will be awarded.

HOW IS IT MARKED?

This answer would gain 5 marks because it makes two different points, and both points have extra detail. It also refers to a relevant source of Christian belief and teaching.

! REMEMBER…

The 5-mark question is similar to the 4-mark question, so try to make **two different points** and **add extra detail** to each of them.

The additional instruction in the question asks you to **'refer to scripture or another source of Christian belief and teaching in your answer'**. Try to think of a reference to the Bible, the Catechism, the words of a prayer or a quotation from a saint, pope or bishop that can back up one of your points. You only need one reference but can add more than one if you want.

Activity

2 Explain **two** of the Church's teachings on the end of time.

Refer to scripture or another source of Christian belief and teaching in your answer. **[5 marks]**

The sample answer below would get 5 marks because there are two points, both with extra detail, and a reference to a source of Christian belief and teaching. Add a tick next to each point. Then underline where each point has extra detail. Finally, draw a circle around a reference to Christian belief and teaching.

The first teaching is that at the end of time, God does not send people to hell. People who go to hell do so because they have rejected God and so it is their own choice. The Catechism of the Catholic Church says that 'For hell, a wilful turning away from God is necessary.'

The second teaching is that no one knows when the end of time will happen, so they should prepare throughout their lives. This preparation includes following Jesus' teachings, including love your neighbour.

TIP

You don't need to quote a source of Christian belief and teaching word-for-word, but try to say where it came from. For example, whether it came from the Bible, a document produced by the Church, a speech by the Pope, etc.

3 Explain **two** styles of music used in worship.

Refer to scripture or another source of Christian belief and teaching in your answer.　　　**[5 marks]**

The sample answer below would get 4 marks as there are two points with extra detail. Try to gain the maximum of 5 marks by adding a source of Christian belief and teaching to either of the points – it doesn't matter which.

One style of music used in worship is a contemporary worship song ✓ **(1)** which is sung by the congregation, often accompanied on more modern instruments like guitars and drums rather than an organ. ✓ **(1)**

_____

_____

More traditional hymns are also used, ✓ **(1)** because they help people to praise God using words they learnt when they were young and which they are used to. They are often accompanied on an organ. ✓ **(1)**

_____

_____

TIP

Here, your source of Christian belief and teaching could be an example of a hymn.

4 Explain **two** ways that Jesus is seen as source of moral teaching.

Refer to scripture or another source of Christian belief and teaching in your answer.　　　**[5 marks]**

The sample answer below would get 2 marks as there is one point with extra detail. Complete the answer by adding a second point with extra detail, as well as a reference to a source of Christian belief and teaching (this can be added to either point).

Firstly, Jesus is seen as a source of moral teaching through his actions. ✓ **(1)**
For example, he was always kind to others and helped those in need. ✓ **(1)**

_____

_____

_____

Secondly... _____

_____

_____

_____

_____

TIP

You don't need to quote a source of Christian belief and teaching word-for-word, but try to say where it came from. For example, whether it came from the Bible, a document produced by the Church, a speech by the Pope, etc.

5 Explain **two** Christian views on salvation.

Refer to scripture or another source of Christian belief and teaching in your answer. **[5 marks]**

_____

_____

_____

_____

_____

_____

_____

_____

_____

_____

6 Explain **two** ways in which Christians understand the nature of God.

Refer to scripture or another source of Christian belief and teaching in your answer. **[5 marks]**

_____

_____

_____

_____

_____

_____

_____

_____

_____

_____

Test the 12-mark question

Example

1 'The resurrection of Jesus is more important than his ascension.'

Evaluate this statement.

In your answer you should:

- give reasoned arguments to support this statement
- give reasoned arguments to support a different point of view
- refer to Christian teaching
- reach a justified conclusion.

[12 marks]
[+3 SPaG marks]

WHAT WILL THE QUESTION LOOK LIKE?

The 12-mark question will always ask you to **evaluate** a statement. The bullet points underneath the statement will tell you the things the examiner expects to see in your answer. Here, you need to give reasoned arguments for and against the statement, and refer to Christian teaching. The final bullet will always ask you to 'reach a justified conclusion'.

HOW IS IT MARKED?

The examiner will mark your answer using level descriptors (see below).

In addition, 3 extra marks will be awarded for your **spelling, punctuation and grammar** (SPaG), and your use of **specialist terminology**. In the exam, your best SPaG mark will be added to your total.

! REMEMBER...

Evaluating means to make a judgement, using **evidence** to decide how convincing you find the statement to be.

You should consider **arguments in support of the statement**, and decide how convincing you think those are, giving at least one reason. You then need to consider **why some people might support a different point of view**, and decide how convincing they are, again giving at least one reason.

You might want to decide how convincing an argument is by considering where it comes from. Is it based on a source of Christian belief and teaching, such as a teaching from the Bible, or something advised by a religious leader such as the Pope? If so, you may decide this evidence strengthens the argument and therefore whether you would support or oppose the statement in the question.

You might decide an argument is weak because it is only a personal opinion, or a popular idea with no strong evidence to support it. This would make it difficult for you to use to support or oppose the statement.

To reach a **justified conclusion** you should consider both sides of the argument, and make your own judgement about which you find more convincing. You might conclude that each side has its own strengths. To make sure your conclusion is 'justified', you need to give **reasons or evidence to support your view**, but don't *just* repeat all the reasons and evidence you have already used.

Level descriptors

Level 1 (1–3 marks)	• Point of view with reason(s) stated in support.
Level 2 (4–6 marks)	• Reasoned consideration of a point of view. • A logical chain of reasoning drawing on knowledge and understanding of relevant evidence and information. OR • Recognition of different points of view, each supported by relevant reasons/evidence. • **Maximum of Level 2 if there is no reference to religion.**
Level 3 (7–9 marks)	• Reasoned consideration of different points of view. • Logical chains of reasoning that draw on knowledge and understanding of relevant evidence and information. • **Clear reference to religion.**
Level 4 (10–12 marks)	• A well-argued response, reasoned consideration of different points of view. • Logical chains of reasoning leading to judgement(s) supported by knowledge and understanding of relevant evidence and information. • **Reference to religion applied to the issue.**

But what is a logical chain of reasoning?

The level descriptors state that to achieve the higher levels you need to show 'logical chains of reasoning' in your answer. This is not as difficult as it sounds. It simply refers to an argument where one idea connects logically to the next.

If you take an idea, develop it by giving more detail and explanation, then provide evidence that supports your idea, you will be demonstrating a logical chain of reasoning. Each step in your argument is a link: together they make a chain of reasoning.

This might already be part of your normal way of writing, even if the phrase is new to you.

You will find some examples in the sample answers that follow.

---

2 'Different styles of music in worship help people to show the glory of God.'

Evaluate this statement.

In your answer you should:

- give reasoned arguments to support this statement
- give reasoned arguments to support a different point of view
- refer to Christian teaching
- reach a justified conclusion.

[12 marks]
[+3 SPaG marks]

Here are four sample answers to the question above. Each one would be awarded a different level. Read all four answers carefully and compare them with the level descriptors on page 132.

Level 1 sample answer

This is a Level 1 answer because:
- it expresses an opinion
- it gives a reason.

To improve this answer the student could:
- create a simple chain of reasoning by giving relevant examples
- include a different point of view with reasons.

I agree that different styles of music help people to show the glory of God. This is because many styles of music are quite beautiful and meaningful, which shows respect to God.

TIP

Here the student mentions 'different styles of music' but doesn't give any examples of these different styles (such as hymns, psalms, modern worship songs, etc.). Adding in some examples would help to improve their answer.

Level 2 sample answer

This is a Level 2 answer because:

- it adds a little more reasoning and evidence
- it mentions a different point of view.

To improve this answer the student could:

- add more reasons
- use a logical chain of reasoning for each point of view.

I agree that different styles of music help people to show the glory of God. This is because many styles of music are quite beautiful and meaningful, which shows respect to God. Different styles of music can be used in different situations.

Young people prefer more modern styles of music and it is best to show glory to God in music you like, so some people might say you should only use modern music in church.

TIP

Look how the student has started to extend their reasoning here. If they want to reach a higher level they could add more detail to this chain of reasoning.

TIP

You might find it helps to structure your answer so all of the arguments to support the statement are grouped together, and all of the arguments to support a different view are grouped together — as the student has done here.

Level 3 sample answer

This is a Level 3 answer because:

- there is a reasoned consideration of different points of view
- it contains chains of reasoning
- it includes a justified conclusion.

To improve this answer the student could:

- provide more detail in the chains of reasoning
- develop the conclusion further.

I agree that different styles of music help people to show the glory of God. This is because many styles of music are quite beautiful and meaningful, which shows respect to God. Different styles of music can be used in different situations, like an old chant for a serious situation or a new hymn for a happy situation. Also it doesn't really matter what style of music is used because the words having meaning is more important than what the music sounds like.

Young people prefer more modern styles of music and it is best to show glory to God in music you like, so some young people might say you should only use modern music in church. But it is a fact that for many churches, a large percentage of the congregation are older. Either way, age shouldn't really matter. The idea that God is eternal and therefore can appreciate different styles of music is an important one. Anyway, some of the more beautiful old-fashioned music is sung by choirs containing many young people who are choristers.

My conclusion is that if the music contains words that are written to glorify God it doesn't matter whether the music is old-fashioned or modern, because the words are most important.

TIP

The student has written a successful chain of reasoning here that builds on the idea that different musical styles show the glory of God. The idea is developed with further reasons, evidence and detail, then summarised neatly.

TIP

To write a Level 3 answer, you need to show 'clear reference to religion'. This can be achieved by using accurate technical terms (such as 'hymn') and including clear beliefs about God or other aspects of a religion (such as the idea that God is eternal).

TIP

The student has written a justified conclusion, expressing a judgement and giving a reason for why they have reached that judgement. Including the word 'because' is always helpful to show this.

Level 4 sample answer

This is a Level 4 answer because:

- it is well argued
- it contains extra points, reasons and evidence that build on the chains of reasoning in the Level 3 answer.

I agree that different styles of music help people to show the glory of God. This is because many styles of music are quite beautiful and meaningful, which shows respect to God. Different styles of music can be used in different situations, like an old chant for a serious situation or a new hymn for a happy situation. It doesn't really matter if the music is new or old, because the words having meaning is more important than what the music sounds like.

Young people prefer more modern styles of music and it is best to show glory to God in music you like, so some young people might say you should only use modern music in church. But it is a fact that for many churches, a large percentage of the congregation are older. Either way, age shouldn't really matter. The idea that God is eternal and therefore can appreciate different styles of music is an important one. It supports the statement that different styles in worship help show God's glory – worshippers have been praising God in different styles for centuries. It is also worth considering that some of the more beautiful old-fashioned music is sung by choirs containing many young people who are choristers. I think it as easy to show glory to God by singing an old hymn accompanied by an organ as it is with a religious song accompanied by a guitar and drums. It is the intention to show glory to God that matters, not the style of music, although if updating music brings more people to God then it must be a good thing.

Some of the most old-fashioned music used in worship is the psalms. These are taken from the Bible, so taking the trouble to put God's words to music and singing them shows the glory of God. Psalm 23, 'The Lord is my Shepherd', is used a lot, especially at funerals. Over the years, old music that shows glory to God has survived. If it didn't show glory to God, it wouldn't have survived. Maybe in a hundred years, some of the more modern music will have been forgotten, but some of it will have been remembered because it was really good.

My conclusion is that if the music contains words that are written to glorify God, it doesn't matter whether the music is old-fashioned or modern, because the words are most important. Choosing to sing them or listen to them means that you want to show the glory of God.

TIP

Look at the sentence openers in the second paragraph 'But it is a fact...' and 'Either way...'. Each sentence links and builds on what has been argued before, rather than stating a list of separate facts. This is a key part of a chain of reasoning – linking points together to form a stronger argument.

TIP

This is a well-written response, including detailed evidence to back up each side of the argument. The student has evaluated the arguments for each side throughout the answer, which can also be a useful way of helping you reach a justified conclusion.

TIP

The student has shown reasoned evaluation in this final sentence of paragraph 2.

TIP

The student has used specific examples, such as Psalm 23, which is a clear reference to religion.

Activity

3 'It is only possible for people to follow the requirement to "love your neighbour" if they care for the environment.'

Evaluate this statement.

In your answer you should:

- give reasoned arguments to support this statement
- give reasoned arguments to support a different point of view
- refer to Christian teaching
- reach a justified conclusion.

[12 marks]
[+3 SPaG marks]

A Read the sample answer below.

I think this statement is good because the environment is what God uses to sustain life. We have a duty of stewardship which means we have to look after the environment for God. This comes from the Genesis creation story. If the environment is protected it makes life much easier for the people who live on the earth.

'Love your neighbour' is a command from Luke's Gospel which means that we should care for all people who are in need of help. It applies to everybody in the world, not just those who live close to where we live ourselves. This means that we should be loving on a global level because if areas of the world that are currently poor are given help to use the earth's resources carefully, they will be able to look after themselves more easily. Therefore caring for the environment by using its resources more carefully is part of 'love your neighbour' and a responsibility that humans should keep.

On the other hand, although love your neighbour can operate on a global level, the duty of stewardship means that we should care for people locally rather than globally. This may not necessarily have anything to do with caring for the global environment but it is loving and it is necessary for poor people at home. Giving money to the homeless is a good action and follows love your neighbour but has nothing to do with the environment. You could argue that building a large hostel to house the homeless is loving but if it is built on green space which has to be cleared of trees, it is not caring for the environment even though it is helping people who have nowhere to live. After all, Genesis says that 'humans have dominion over all other creatures' so in some cases, we can help people even if it is not great for the environment.

I therefore disagree that it is only possible for people to follow the requirement to 'love your neighbour' if they care for the environment because there are examples of using the quotation to help people locally in ways which may harm the environment. Such arguments are not very convincing though but they are possible. However, it is an ideal that Christians should try to work towards, after all, everything God created was good so we should try to keep it that way.

B Now answer the following questions about the sample answer on the previous page.

1. What is the main argument used by the student to support the statement?

    _____

    _____

    _____

2. Do you agree that this is a strong argument? Why or why not?

    _____

    _____

    _____

3. Summarise the argument against the statement.

    _____

    _____

    _____

4. Do you think the example about building a hostel is a good one? Why or why not?

    _____

    _____

    _____

5. Which argument do you think is strongest? Why?

    _____

    _____

    _____

6. Using a coloured pen, highlight any references to Christian teaching that you can find (which the question asks for in the third bullet point).

    Circle any part where the student gives a personal judgement.

    Underline any phrases where the student demonstrates evaluation.

4 'The Parable of the Rich Man and Lazarus shows what the afterlife is like.'

Evaluate this statement.

In your answer you should:

- give reasoned arguments to support this statement
- give reasoned arguments to support a different point of view
- refer to Christian teaching
- reach a justified conclusion.

[12 marks]
[+3 SPaG marks]

The answer below is a Level 1 answer because it gives a point of view and has a couple of simple reasons to support it. In the space below, turn this into a Level 2 answer. You could do this by either:

- explaining further how the parable shows what it is like for Lazarus in heaven and what it is like for the rich man in hell, to turn what the student has written into a 'logical chain of reasoning'

or:

- adding a different point of view, with a simple reason to support it.

I agree that the story of the Rich Man and Lazarus shows what the afterlife is like because it shows what it is like for Lazarus in heaven and also for the rich man in hell.

_____

_____

_____

_____

_____

_____

_____

_____

_____

_____

_____

_____

_____

_____

_____

_____

_____

_____

Now rewrite your answer so it is likely to achieve Level 3. To do this, you should:

- provide reasons and evidence to support the statement. Which bits in the parable help to show what the afterlife is like?

- provide reasons and evidence to support a different point of view. How does the parable fail to show what the afterlife is like?

- include a clear reference to religion. For example, you could include some facts about what Christians believe happens in the afterlife, to support your arguments for or against the statement.

TIP

Try to include logical chains of reasoning in your answer (see page 132)

I agree that the story of the Rich Man and Lazarus shows what the afterlife is like because it shows what it is like for Lazarus in heaven and also for the rich man in hell.

_____

_____

_____

_____

_____

_____

_____

_____

_____

_____

_____

_____

_____

_____

_____

_____

_____

_____

_____

_____

_____

_____

_____

5 'God as creator is the most important Christian belief about the nature of God.'

Evaluate this statement.

In your answer you should:

- give reasoned arguments to support this statement
- give reasoned arguments to support a different point of view
- refer to Christian teaching
- reach a justified conclusion.

[12 marks]
[+3 SPaG marks]

 REMEMBER...

Focus your answer on the statement you are asked to evaluate.

- Try to write at least three paragraphs – one with arguments to support the statement, one with arguments to support a different point of view, and a final paragraph with a justified conclusion stating which side you think is more convincing, and why.

- Look at the bullet points in the question, and make sure you include everything that they ask for.

- The key skill that you need to demonstrate is evaluation. This means expressing judgements on the arguments that support or oppose the statement, based on evidence. You might decide an argument is strong because it is based on a source of religious belief and teaching, such as a teaching from the Bible, or because it is based on scientific evidence. You might decide an argument is weak because it is based on a personal opinion, or a popular idea with no scientific basis. You can use phrases in your chains of reasoning such as 'I think this a convincing argument because…' or 'In my opinion, this is a weak argument because…'.

6 'Evangelism can be made more effective by the use of drama.'

Evaluate this statement.

In your answer you should:

- give reasoned arguments to support this statement
- give reasoned arguments to support a different point of view
- refer to Christian teaching
- reach a justified conclusion.

[12 marks]
[+3 SPaG marks]

_____

_____

_____

_____

_____

_____

_____

_____

_____

_____

_____

_____

_____

_____

_____

_____

_____

_____

_____

_____

_____

_____

_____

OXFORD
UNIVERSITY PRESS

Great Clarendon Street, Oxford, OX2 6DP, United Kingdom

Oxford University Press is a department of the University of Oxford. It furthers the University's objective of excellence in research, scholarship, and education by publishing worldwide. Oxford is a registered trade mark of Oxford University Press in the UK and in certain other countries

British Library Cataloguing in Publication Data

Data available

978-0-19-844496-1

3 5 7 9 10 8 6 4 2

Paper used in the production of this book is a natural, recyclable product made from wood grown in sustainable forests.

The manufacturing process conforms to the environmental regulations of the country of origin.

Printed in China by Leo Paper Products Ltd.

Acknowledgements

We are grateful to the authors and publishers for use of extracts from their titles and in particular for the following:

The Scripture quotations contained herein are from **New Revised Standard Version Bible**, copyright © 1989 National Council of the Churches of Christ in the United States of America. Used by permission. All rights reserved worldwide; One Scripture quotation contained herein from **Revised Standard Version of the Bible—Second Catholic Edition (Ignatius Edition)** Copyright © 2006 National Council of the Churches of Christ in the United States of America. Used by permission. All rights reserved worldwide; Excerpt from the English translation of **Non-Biblical Readings from The Liturgy of the Hours** © 1973, 1974, 1975, International Commission on English in the Liturgy Corporation (ICEL). Reproduced with permission; Excerpts from **Catechism of the Catholic Church**, http://www.vatican.va/archive/ccc_css/archive/catechism/ccc_toc.htm (Strathfield, NSW: St Pauls, 2000). © Libreria Editrice Vaticana. Reproduced with permission from The Vatican; Excerpt from the English translation of **Pastoral Care of the Sick: Rites of Anointing and Viaticum** © 1982, International Commission on English in the Liturgy Corporation. All rights reserved. Reproduced with permission; **AQA:** *GCSE Religious Studies B, Paper 1: Catholic Christianity* (AQA 2017). Reproduced with permission from AQA; **Julian of Norwich:** *Love's Trinity: a companion to Julian of Norwich*, translated by John-Julian. (Liturgical Press, 2009). Copyright 2009 by Order of Saint Benedict. Reproduced with permission from Liturgical Press; **Pope Benedict XVI:** *Verbum Domini*, On the Word of God in the Life and Mission of the Church, September 30th 2010 (The Vatican, 2010). © Libreria Editrice Vaticana. Reproduced with permission from The Vatican; **Pope Francis:** *Laudato Si*, May 24th 2015, (The Vatican, 2015). © Libreria Editrice Vaticana. Reproduced with permission from The Vatican; **Pope Paul VI:** *Dei Verbum*, Dogmatic Constitution on Divine Revelation, November 18th 1965 (The Vatican, 1965). © Libreria Editrice Vaticana. Reproduced with permission from The Vatican; *Gaudium et Spes*, Pastoral Constitution on the Church in the Modern World, December 7th, 1965 (The Vatican, 1965). © Libreria Editrice Vaticana. Reproduced with permission from The Vatican; *Inter Mirifica*, Decree on the Media of Social Communications, December 4th 1963 (The Vatican, 1963). © Libreria Editrice Vaticana. Reproduced with permission from The Vatican; *Lumen Gentium,* Dogmatic Constitution on the Church, November 21st 1964 (The Vatican, 1964). Reproduced with permission from The Vatican. © Libreria Editrice Vaticana.

Cover: Hands of God and Adam, detail from The Creation of Adam, from the Sistine Ceiling, 1511 (fresco) (pre restoration), Buonarroti, Michelangelo (1475-1564)/Vatican Museums and Galleries, Vatican City/Bridgeman Images

Illustrations: Jason Ramasami and Q2A Media Services Pvt. Ltd.

Photos: p4: 123RF/Cosmin-Constantin Sava; **p5:** Godong/Universal Images Group/Getty Images; **p25:** Aurelian Images/Alamy; **p32:** Catherine Leblanc/Godong/Getty Images; **p35:** World History Archive/Alamy; **p47:** Hollygraphic/Shutterstock; **p78:** age fotostock/Alamy; **p100:** giulio napolitano/Shutterstock; **p105:** World History Archive/Alamy; **p117:** Agencja Fotograficzna Caro/Alamy; **p119:** Godong/Alamy.

Although we have made every effort to trace and contact all copyright holders before publication this has not been possible in all cases. If notified, the publisher will rectify any errors or omissions at the earliest opportunity.

Links to third party websites are provided by Oxford in good faith and for information only. Oxford disclaims any responsibility for the materials contained in any third party website referenced in this work.

Please note that the practice questions in this book allow students a genuine attempt at practising exam skills, but they are not intended to replicate examination papers.

Thank you

OUP wishes to thank Matthew Dell and Julie Haigh for their help reviewing this book.

What Do We Know About Separating Mixtures

Materials and objects are often made up of several things, for example:

- an egg has a yolk and white
- salt water is a mixture of water and salt
- we mix flour and sugar when we make sweet pastry
- a path can be made from sand and gravel.

1a Think of three other mixtures of solids.

1b Think of three other liquids that are mixtures.

Sometimes we need to split things into their individual parts.

Farmers need to remove stones from soil to grow better crops.

Factories create dried milk from liquid milk by separating out the liquid, as milk powder is milk with the water removed.

2 Can we use the same process to separate stones from soil as we do to separate water from milk? Explain your answer.

The children in nursery class have been playing with sand and water, but they have now got sand in their water tray.

 3 How could you help the children to separate the sand and water?

Sieving

We use **sieves** to separate things. When you were young you might have played with sieves in the sand and water tray. A sieve has holes of a certain size. We can use sieves to separate two solids with different-sized bits or particles. If we choose the right sieve, one solid will go through the holes and the other will not.

Word box
sieve

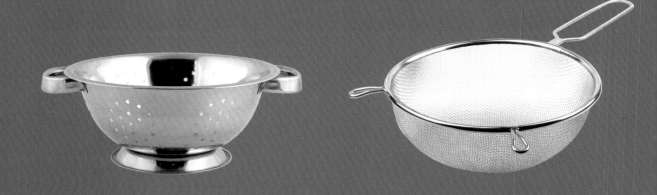

1 What are these two pieces of kitchen equipment called?
2 Why do you think most kitchens have both types?

Using kitchen sieves

You will need: the kitchen equipment in the pictures on page 2 and a small amount of flour, sugar, tea leaves, coffee, dried rice

Work in a small group and try sieving each with both sieves. Before you do this, answer the questions below.

1 Which substances do you think will pass through both sieves?

2a Which substance do you think will only pass through one of the sieves?

2b State which sieve you think it will pass through.

2c Why will it not pass through the other sieve?

Now carry out tests to find out if your answers are correct.

B

A

C

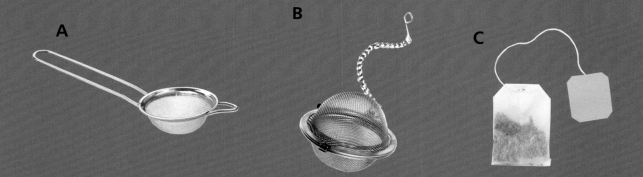

3a What are these three items used for?

3b Why are they like a sieve?

3c Which do you think is best? Explain your answer.

More Uses For Sieving

Sieves do not all have the same-sized holes. A set of **graduated** sieves is a collection of several sieves each with different-sized holes. These are used to separate a few different substances in a mixture.

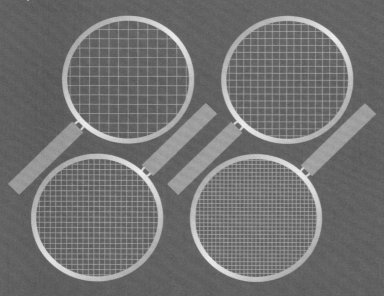

Graduated sieves need to be stacked in the correct order. The sieves should gradually have smaller and smaller holes as you move down the stack.

When used correctly there will be a different substance on top of the mesh of each sieve.

1 Why do the sieves need to be stacked in a particular order?

2 Where do you think you place the mixture? Why?

There are many different kinds of seeds and these are of many sizes.

3 How would you use graduated sieves to separate a bag of four different types of seeds? Each seed is a different size.
Record a set of instructions.

Industrial Sieving

Sieves are not just used for household jobs. There are some much bigger sieves that are used in **industry**.

Word box
industry

Enormous sieves are used in water treatment plants. Sieving is the first thing that happens in a series of steps to get water clean enough to drink. Sieving takes out larger objects, for example tissue, from the water.

Farmers also use sieves to make sure they end up with just the grain when they harvest crops. The grain goes through the holes and the unwanted bits of the plants are left behind in the sieve.

1a Find out about other industrial uses for sieves. List these.

1b Choose one and make an information leaflet about it.

Dissolving

Some solids will **dissolve** in some liquids. Dissolved means the solid and the liquid have mixed together well, and the pieces of the solid are so small that we cannot see them anymore. When a solid is dissolved in a liquid the bits of the solid are spread out through the liquid, and a **solution** is formed.

A cup of very sweet coffee

You will need: a teaspoon, instant coffee, sugar, a transparent mug, very warm water

Work in a small group.

1 Fill the mug to three-quarters full with the warm water.

2 Add four teaspoons of sugar. What do you observe?

3 Stir the mixture. What do you observe?

4 Add a teaspoon of coffee and stir again. What do you observe now?

1 Record and explain your observations for the activity above.

If a solid dissolves in a liquid we say it is **soluble**. If a solid does not dissolve in a liquid we say it is **insoluble**.

How much sugar will dissolve in cold water?

You will need: a teaspoon, sugar, a transparent measuring beaker, 100 cm³ water

Work in a small group.

1 Add the water to the beaker.

2 Add the sugar a teaspoon at a time.

3 Stir the mixture after each teaspoon of sugar is added. Check to make sure it has dissolved before adding the next one.

4 Count how many teaspoons of sugar you have added before the sugar no longer dissolves.

5 How many teaspoons of sugar dissolved?

6a What happened to the water level as the sugar was dissolving?

6b Can you explain why?

7 Why do you think the sugar stopped dissolving?

Predict it!

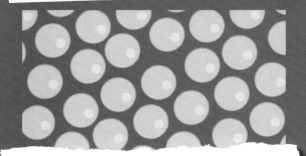

Particles of a liquid, such as water.

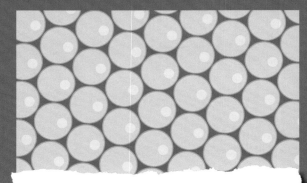

Particles of a solid, such as sugar.

Scientists often use models to explain what is happening. We know everything is made of particles. The diagrams above show a model for what water and sugar would look like if we could see the particles they are made of.

Some of these foods are soluble in water and others are not.

1 **Talk to a partner. Predict whether the food will dissolve in water or not. Record your predictions.**

You will need: the foods in the diagram, water, six transparent cups, six teaspoons

Work in a small group.

1 Half-fill the cups with water and add a teaspoon of each food stuff to a separate cup of water.

2 Stir each mixture. Observe what happens.

3 Record your results and check to see whether the results match your predictions.

2 What happens when a solid dissolves in water?

3 Draw and write an explanation of what happens when a solid does *not* dissolve in water and instead sinks.

4 Draw and write an explanation of what happens when a solid does *not* dissolve in water and instead floats.

Solids can be soluble in one type of liquid but not in another. Another liquid we use in the kitchen is cooking oil.

5 How is cooking oil similar to and different from water?

Which foods dissolve in oil?

You will need: the foods in the diagram on page 8, cooking oil, six transparent cups, six teaspoons, paper towels

Work in a small group.

1 Half-fill the six cups with oil.

2 Predict which food stuffs will dissolve in cooking oil. Write down your predictions.

3 Add a teaspoon of each food stuff to a separate cup of oil. Stir each mixture and observe and record what happens.

4 Do your results match your predictions?

More About Dissolving

We can investigate many different things about substances dissolving. These diagrams show a simple comparative test that Ajay's group decided to carry out.

Discuss with a partner.

1 What do you think Ajay's group were trying to find out?

2 Look at the diagrams. What is different when baby oil is dropped on to the candy floss?

3 Why do you think this happens?

Scientists carry out fair tests to answer scientific questions. We call these tests 'investigations'. The questions that require this type of test mean we must only change one thing during the investigation. We measure another change and keep all other variables the same.

For example, if we wanted to investigate whether salt dissolves more quickly in hot water than in cold water, we would need to change only the temperature of the water. We would measure the time it took for the salt to dissolve. We would need to keep the volume of water, mass of salt and amount of stirring the same. This would be a fair test.

4 Discuss with a partner some other possible investigations linked to dissolving. Write these down.

Investigate it!

Identical sugar mice were put into different temperature baths that each contained the same volume of water.

This graph shows how long it took each sugar mouse to dissolve.

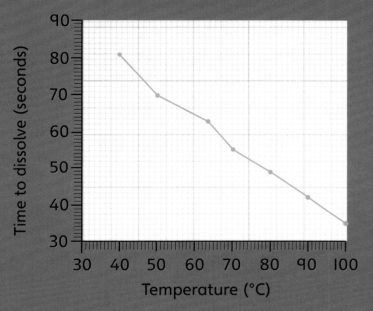

1 Work with a partner to sort the questions below into two groups: those we can and those we cannot answer using the graph.

A In which temperature water did the mouse dissolve in the least time?

B Do pink mice dissolve as quickly as white ones?

C How much longer did it take a mouse to dissolve at 75°C than at 90°C?

D Will stirring the water speed up the time taken for the mice to dissolve?

E How quickly will a mouse dissolve at 20°C?

2 Write down two more questions that can be answered using the graph.

Evaporation

Ayesha is using water to paint on sugar paper.

Word box
evaporate

Sugar paper is very absorbent, so soaks up the water easily. If she leaves the picture in the sunshine the water will quickly **evaporate** and the picture will disappear. Evaporation happens when a liquid becomes a gas through heating.

Wet and dry sugar paper

You will need: a bowl of water, two strips of coloured (not black or white) sugar paper

1 Put one strip of sugar paper in the water and leave it for 1 minute.

2 Pull it out and then lay the two pieces of sugar paper next to each other.

3 Do the two pieces of paper look different? Why do they look different?

4 What will happen if you leave the wet piece of paper in a warm, dry place overnight? Why does this happen?

Water painting

You will need: a large piece of craft paper, a paint brush, water, a piece of sugar paper

1 Lay the sugar paper on the craft paper. Use the paint brush dipped in water to water paint your own simple picture on the piece of sugar paper.

2 Record how your picture changes every half hour for three hours.

After a heavy shower there are often puddles on the ground but these quickly seem to disappear. Class 5 have some ideas about what happens to the puddles.

Here are their ideas:

They soak into the ground.

Teachers mop them up.

Animals drink them.

They change from liquid water to water vapour and are in the air.

1 Discuss with a partner what you think happens to the puddles in your school playground after it has rained. Explain your answer.

The teacher assures them that no animals are allowed in the school grounds and the puddles are not mopped up. This means the water either evaporates or soaks into the ground.

2 Discuss with a partner how you would find out if puddles evaporate.

Write your plan for how you would investigate this. Make sure you explain how you would ensure that the water does not soak into the ground.

Investigating Evaporation

These pictures show what has happened to brown sugar solution left on a saucer for four days.

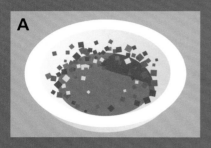

A

C

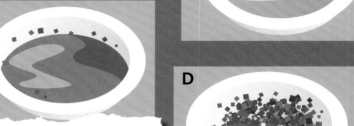

B

D

The brown sugar solution was photographed each day, but the photos have been mixed up.

 1 Draw these diagrams in the correct order to show the sugar solution on days one to four.

Does heat affect evaporation?

You will need: a cup, 100 cm³ cold water, two saucers, brown sugar, a dessertspoon

Work in a small group.

1 Dissolve five dessertspoons of sugar in a cup of 100 cm³ cold water to make a sugar solution.

2 Place two spoonfuls of sugar solution on each saucer.

3a Put one saucer in a fridge (or somewhere cool). Put the other one somewhere warm. Leave them for two days.

3b What do you think will happen? Why?

4 Observe both saucers of sugar solution. Which one has evaporated more?

Keep the rest of the sugar solution for the next activity.

Ninety-eight per cent of a jellyfish's body is water. If they are washed up on a hot beach, they can almost completely disappear!

2 Why do you think this happens to a jellyfish?

Nadia's hairdryer is only blowing cold air. She wonders whether it will dry her hair faster than just leaving it to dry.

3 Do you think Nadia's hair will dry faster with the hairdryer? Explain your answer.

How does moving air affect evaporation?

You will need: the cup of sugar solution, a dessertspoon, two saucers, a fan

Work in a small group.

1 Place two spoonfuls of sugar solution on each saucer.

2a Put one saucer in a place where the air is still. Put the other one in front of the fan on a low setting so it gently blows air over the saucer. Leave them for two hours.

2b Which do you think will evaporate quicker? Why?

3 Observe both saucers of sugar solution. Which one has evaporated more?

15

Understanding Evaporation

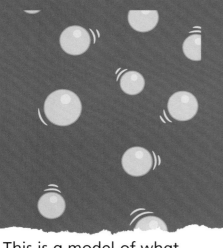

This is a model of what particles look like in a gas.

1 How is this particle model different from the particle model for a liquid?

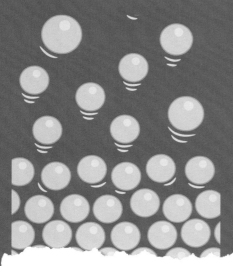

During evaporation: All the particles in a liquid move but some move more and escape the liquid.

Slippery spheres

You will need: a cup of water, a few slippery spheres

Slippery spheres. These are often used by florists at the bottom of a vase of flowers.

Work in a pair.

1 Put the slippery spheres in the cup of water and leave them overnight.

What has happened to the spheres? Why?

2 Take the spheres out of the water and leave them in a warm place in a saucer. Look at the spheres every day.

What happens? Why?

3 Draw a particle diagram to show what happens when the spheres absorb the water.

You have found out a lot about evaporation.

Read the statements below then discuss with a partner which statements are true.

A   Evaporation happens when a liquid becomes a gas.

B   Evaporation increases if it is cooler.

C   Evaporation increases if it is windier.

D   Evaporation can happen at any temperature even if the liquid is frozen.

2 Record whether you think each statement is true or false and give a reason for your answer.

Some countries can suffer with unexpected heavy rainfall and flooding. Water may rush into houses and specialist companies come and dry out the carpets.

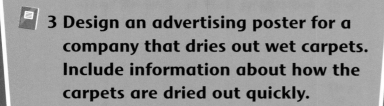

3 Design an advertising poster for a company that dries out wet carpets. Include information about how the carpets are dried out quickly.

Filtration

Filtration is another way of separating a mixture. It is another type of sieving. It uses a piece of paper or fabric with tiny holes or **pores** as the sieve. This is called a **filter**. When you pour a mixture of a liquid and a solid through the filter, the liquid goes through the tiny holes but the solid is left behind.

This diagram shows equipment that is often used in a classroom to filter dirty water.

Word box
filter
filtration
pores

1 The labels for the beaker, clean water, dirty water, dirt, filter paper and funnel have been left off the diagram. Draw and label a diagram for filtering dirty water.

2 Record instructions on how to filter dirty water. In your instructions make it clear what each piece of equipment is for.

choosing a filter paper

You will need: a bottle of dirty water, a funnel, a beaker, cling film, kitchen roll, a piece of fabric/cloth, metal foil

Work in a small group.

1 Use a magnifying glass and look more closely at these materials. Which materials do you think will filter the dirty water? Why? Which do you think will *not* filter the water? Why not? Record your predictions.

Cling film

Kitchen roll

A piece of cloth

Metal foil

2 Carry out a test to find out which materials will filter the dirty water and record your findings.

3 List three other materials you could use to filter dirty water.

4 If you filtered dirty water but it was still not clean what could you do to make it cleaner? Discuss your ideas in a group. Record all your ideas.

Uses of Filtration

Many of us can get clean water by simply turning on a tap. In some countries access to clean water is not so simple. People have to filter dirty water from lakes and rivers by hand. This takes out the larger particles of dirt but tiny bacteria can pass through the holes in the filter. Even though the water looks clean it can make people ill.

There are organisations that help so that more people have clean water.

1 Research an organisation that is trying to make sure people have clean water. Write a leaflet to encourage people to find out more about the organisation's work.

A filter can also be used to separate solid particles from a gas. Most air conditioning units use a filter. As the air goes through the unit the filter traps the solid particles in the air but lets the clean air pass through.

2 With a partner, research other places that you might find an air filter. List as many as you can.

Granulated sugar

Icing sugar

Sugar is used to sweeten food and drink. There are many different kinds. Icing sugar is very useful for cake makers. It is used to make icing for the tops of cakes.

3 Look closely at these pictures. What is the difference between the granulated sugar and the icing sugar?

4 What do you think will happen to icing sugar if you add it to water?

icing sugar

You will need: a transparent plastic cup of water, icing sugar, a teaspoon, a hand lens

Work in a pair.

1 Add the teaspoon of icing sugar to the water. What do you observe? Why?

2 Use the hand lens to look closely on the top of the water. What do you observe? What do you think this is? Why do you think it is there?

3 How would you separate the mixture of icing sugar and water?

Techniques to Separate Mixtures

Everybody accidentally spills things sometimes. **Separation techniques** are often a good way to put things right.

1 Look at these diagrams closely; they show some mistakes where different things have become mixed. Discuss with a partner how you would use a separation technique to put each one right.

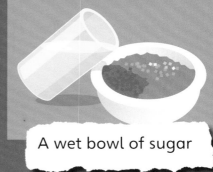

A wet bowl of sugar

A broken tea bag

Peppercorns in the flour

Mixed up pins and matches

Wrong bottle

2 Think of some other mix-ups that could be put right using a separation technique. Draw and describe them.
   Challenge your partner to identify how they would separate them.

The children in Class 5 have been learning about masks. In Class 5's art lesson they have been asked to design a festival mask. They can use any of the equipment in the diagram below. Unfortunately some of the things have got mixed up!

Mask

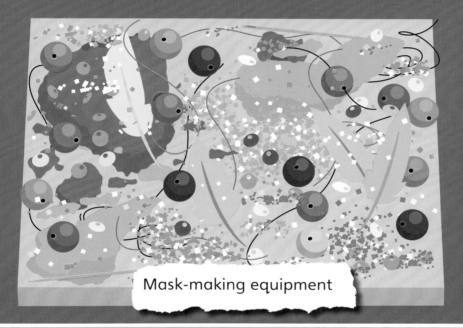
Mask-making equipment

3 With a partner discuss how you would separate the art and craft equipment for these three mix-ups:
- feathers, beads, sequins and glitter.
- glitter, powder paint and thread.
- needles, powder paint and sequins.

Record the separation techniques you would use, as well as the order you would use them in and what would be separated out after each technique.

4 How would you separate a mix-up of *all* the equipment?

23

Glossary

Dissolve a solid and liquid mixing together, such that the bits of the solid are so small they cannot be seen

Evaporate a liquid becoming a gas

Filter paper or fabric with tiny holes (pores) like a sieve, which allows some things to pass through; usually used to separate an insoluble solid from a liquid or tiny solid particle from a gas

Filtration a way of separating a mixture using a filter

Graduated arranged in size order. With graduated sieves the sieve with the largest holes is at the top and the holes in each sieve get smaller from top to bottom

Industry producing and processing materials to make different types of things for people to use

Insoluble a solid that does not dissolve in a liquid is insoluble in that liquid

Pores tiny holes

Separation techniques different methods to take one substance out of a mixture

Sieve a piece of equipment that separates two solids of different-sized particles

Soluble dissolves in a liquid

Solution formed when a solid dissolves completely in a liquid